national archaeological museum of naples

quick guide

edited by
Stefano De Caro

text by
Rosanna Cappelli

national archaeological museum of naples

electa napoli

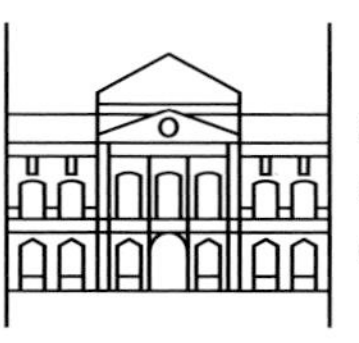

soprintendenza
archeologica
di napoli e caserta

National Archaeological
Museum of Naples

Scientific Directors
Stefano De Caro
Maria Rosaria Borriello

Graphic Archive
Eva Nardella

Photographic Archive
Alessandra Villone

Editorial Services
Marco de Gemmis
Floriana Miele

Commercial Services
Stefania Saviano

Electa Napoli

Scientific Coordinator
Rosanna Cappelli

Managing Editor
Silvia Cassani

Graphic design and layout
Enrica D'Aguanno
Ivana Gaeta

Translations
Globe s.n.c.
Colum Fordham

Image Coordinator
and Museum Layout
JFK

Photographs
Luciano Pedicini (Art Archives);
Photographic Archive of the
Soprintendenza Archeologica
di Napoli a Caserta (Giorgio
Albano, Gaetano Catapano, Nicola
Di Giovanni, Antonio Mannillo,
Stefano Vurruso); Fotografica
Foglia.

We would like to thank Capware of Gaetano Capasso for the virtual image of the House of Punta Chiarito

First english edition September 1999
Printed in Italy

First reprint September 2001

Contents

Transporting the antiquities of Herculaneum from the Museum of Portici to the Palazzo degli Studi in Naples, from the "Voyage pittoresque ou description des Royaumes de Naples et de Sicile" de l'Abbé de Saint-Non, Paris 1781-86

The History of the Museum and its collection of antiquities

In order to reconstruct the complicated historical events that led to the creation of the Museum, we must go back in time to the first half of the 18th century and to the enlightened cultural approach of Charles III of Bourbon who came to the throne of Naples in 1734. From his mother's side (Elizabetta Farnese), he inherited an exceptional collection of works of art and antiquities, which at that time were divided between Naples, Rome (Farnese Palace, Farnesiani Gardens on the Palatine Hills, Villa Farnesina and Villa Madama), and Parma (Ducal Palace of Colorno). During his fifth year on the throne (1738), Charles III of Bourbon commissioned the construction of the Royal Villa of Capodimonte which was destined to house the "Farnese Museum". The year 1738 had begun under a good omen for the King: the prolific excavations of Resina (thirty years earlier, that same area had been investigated by order of Prince d'Elboeuf, uncovering the statues which would later find their way to the family collection of Maria Amalia of Saxony, the wife of Charles III) which led to the discovery of the rich sculptural decorations of the stage of the Theatre of Herculaneum. Ten years later, in 1748, the excavations of Pompeii began followed, in 1749, by those in Stabia: the wealth of material which came forth was housed in the Rooms of the Royal Villa of Portici and became the nucleus of the historical *Herculanean Museum* (1750).
However, the threat of Vesuvius erupting on Portici, and the slow progress being made on the Villa of Capodimonte, convinced the successor of Charles III, Ferdinand IV of

Basement
18-23 Egyptian collection
150-157 Epigraphic collection

Ground Floor
1-7 Great Masters (in the future, Farnese sculptures)
8 Carracci Gallery (in the future, Farnese sculptures)
9-10 Farnese Gems (in the future, Farnese sculptures)
11-16 Baths of Caracalla (in the future, Farnese sculptures)
24-28 Educational Section (in the future, Farnese sculptures)
29 Roman portraits (in the future, Farnese sculptures)
30-34 Exhibition Room
35-45 Sculptures of Roman Campania

Mezzanine Floor
51-56 Numismatics
57-64 Mosaics
65 The Secret Room

First Floor
66-78 The paintings of Pompeii, the stuccoes, the garden
79-84 Temple of Isis
85-89 Bronzes, silver, glass, the arena, the baths, and other finds of the Vesuvian cities
96 Scale Model of Pompeii
114-117 Villa of the Papyri
118-120 Parthenope and Neapolis
121-123 Cumae
124-125 Pithekoussai
126-128 Prehistory and Protohistory
129 Introduction to the Topographic section
130-136 Non-Hellenic populations in Campania
137-144 Magna Graecia

Second Floor
147-149 Prehistory
100-103 Engraved coppers, Greek vases

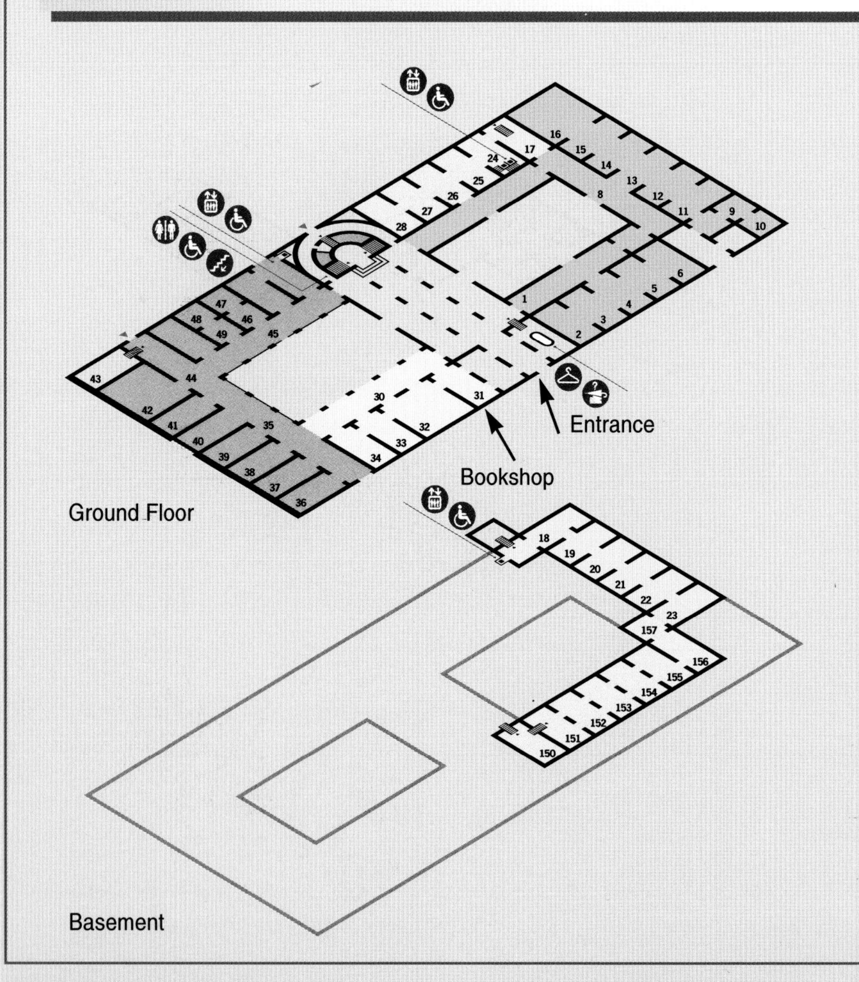

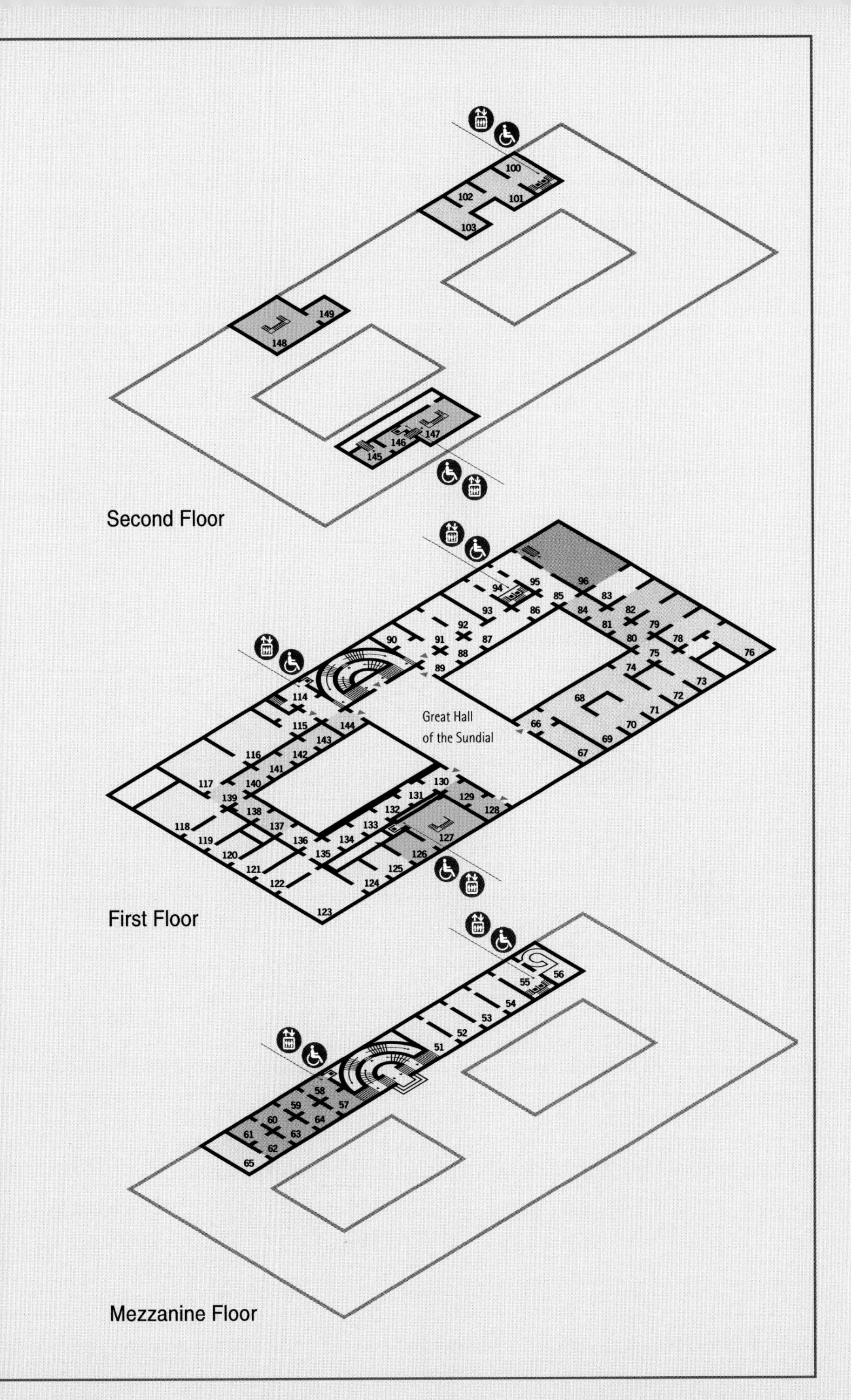
Second Floor
100
101
102
103
148
149
145
146
147
First Floor
Great Hall
of the Sundial
Mezzanine Floor

Bourbon, to unify all the family collections into one magnificent Museum and for this reason, the Palazzo degli Studi of Naples was chosen "for the use of the Royal Museum of Portici, the Picture Gallery of Capodimonte, the grand Public Library, the School of the Three Fine Arts, and the Room for the Study of Nudes". The restructuring of this dilapidated late Renaissance building was assigned to the architect Ferdinando Fuga, later succeeded by Pompeo Schiantarelli, whose idea it was to build an upper floor and the large semi-circle at the back of the building. Increasing the available space coincided with the daring plan, already proposed by Vanvitelli, to transfer the fabulous Roman collection of the Farnese family to Naples. This complicated and costly operation, which began in 1787 and continued for a number of years, was completed by Domenico Venuti, an antique dealer, and by the painter Philipp Hackert. The troubled political situation of those years did not facilitate the completion of the construction work on the new Neapolitan Museum which was inaugurated, after a number of ups and downs, in 1816 with the following name: "Royal Bourbonic Museum". The Museum's subsequent history is linked to Michele Arditi, Francesco Maria Avellino and Giuseppe Fiorelli, the latter being a forerunner of those policies which regard the conservation and sensitive exploitation of the territory which is the basis of the modern conception of a museum of antiquities.
The positivist historian Ettore Pais was in charge of the rearrangement of the collections of the Neapolitan Museum at the turn of the last century, and he did so with an innovative project for the period, which was essentially unchanged until recently.
The transfer of the Picture Gallery to Capodimonte in 1957 gave way to a restructuring still underway today, which is careful to preserve the tradition and prestige of the royal collections, but also to link the Museum more closely to the history and archaeology of the area.

Genealogy of the Bourbons of Naples

Philip V (1683-1746) King of Spain's
second marriage to
Elisabetta Farnese of Parma

Charles (1716-1788) King of Naples
from 1734 to 1759. He became Charles III
of Spain in 1759; he married Maria Amalia
of Saxony in 1738 (d. 1760)

Charles IV
(1748-1819)
King of Spain

Ferdinand IV (1751-1825) King of Naples,
after the second Restoration the King of the
Two Sicilies married Maria Carolina of Austria
(d. 1814), and morganatically Lucia Migliaccio,
Duchess of Floridia (d. 1826)

Francis I (1777-1830) King of the Two Sicilies,
marries Maria Clementina of Austria (d. 1801),
and Isabella of Spain in 1802 (d. 1848)

Ferdinand II (1810-1830) King of the Two Sicilies,
marries Maria Cristina of Savoy (d. 1836), and
Maria Teresa Isabella of Austria in 1837 (d. 1867)

Francis II (1836-1894) King of the Two Sicilies,
marries Maria Sofia of Baviera (d. 1925);
he loses his throne in 1860

The Epigraphic Collection

This collection, which has been recently set up (1995), consists of both material from private collections (of scholars such as Fulvio Orsini, Stefano Borgia, Francesco Daniele, Carlo Maria Rosini), as well as from excavations and discoveries made in Campania and in the other Regions of southern Italy.
The first part of the collection (Room 150) is dedicated to documentation in Greek and the next part (Room 151) to Greek inscriptions from Naples. Next comes evidence of the pre-Roman languages in central-southern Italy (Etruscan, Oscan, Vestian, Volscian) (Rooms 151 and 152); political and institutional epigraphs (Room 153); religious epigraphs (Room 153); lastly, (Rooms 154 and 155) there is a selection of the numerous inscriptions found in the excavations of the Vesuvian cities and the Phlegrean Fields.

Orfic lamina from Thurii

THE TABLETS OF HERACLEA

These were discovered at the beginning of the 18th century in a river bed in the countryside between Eraclea and Metaponto in the Basilicata region; they contain two inscriptions from the end of the 4th-beginning of the 5th centuries B.C. regarding the boundaries and the location of agricultural land belonging to the sanctuaries of Dionysus and Athena Poliade, which had been illegally occupied by private citizens and then redeemed. This document is of extraordinary importance in reconstructing the agrarian economy of the Greek colonies of Ionic Lucania, dominated by the cultivation of cereals (wheat, spelt and, in particular, barley), vines and olives.

SUNDIAL OF THE STABIAN BATHS

The inscription, written in the Oscan language, tells us that the sundial was donated by the quaestor Maras Atinis thanks to the money collected from the payment of fines by the citizens. The first sundial in Rome was brought there from Catania by Marco Valerio Messalla in the year 263 B.C., and was placed in the Comitia of the Republican Forum. Before then, the Comitia itself, which was of regular shape and was oriented according to the cardinal points, was used as an enormous sundial, permitting the heralds to identify the most important moments of the day: dawn, noon and sunset.

The Egyptian Collection

The exhibition gathers together the main parts of various collections, from the eighteenth-century collection belonging to Cardinal Stefano Borgia (purchased in 1815 by Ferdinand IV of Bourbon) (Rooms 18-20), to the more recent ones of the Venetian Giuseppe Picchianti (Rooms 21-22) and the German Schnars (Room 20, display case 15). A specific section is dedicated to illustrating the Egyptian documents discovered in the cities of Campania (Room 21) which testify to the intense relationship between Rome and Egypt, which began in the Ptolemaic period and for the whole of the 2nd century B.C. and the Egyptian styles which spread to the West after the victory of Octavius at Azio (31 B.C.). In terms of the number and quality of display pieces, the Neapolitan collection is second in importance (in Italy) only to the Egyptian Museum of Turin.

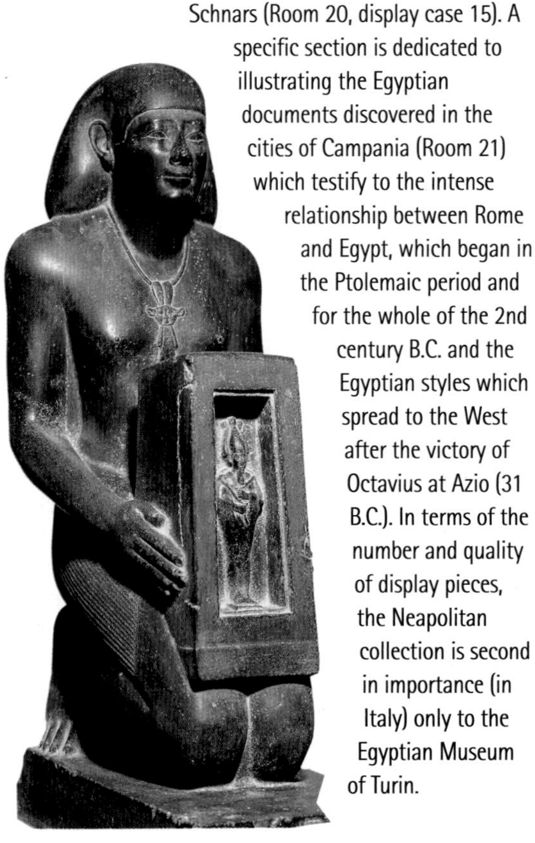

FARNESE NAOFORO

The statue, which is the only Egyptian exemplar from the Farnese Collection, represents a kneeling figure holding an aedicula or small temple (known as a *naos*, hence the name naophoros) in his hands which contains a cult image of the god Osiris with the characteristic atef crown (a tiara between two ostrich feathers), the curved sceptre, and the flabellum. The inscription, which is carved on the rear pillar, allows us to identify the dedicatee as Uah-ib-ra Meryneith, keeper of the royal seals, intimate friend of the King, director of the house of the two crowns, priest of Horus, head of the Dep district, Superintendent of the seals, as well as enabling us to date the monument to the XXVI dynasty.

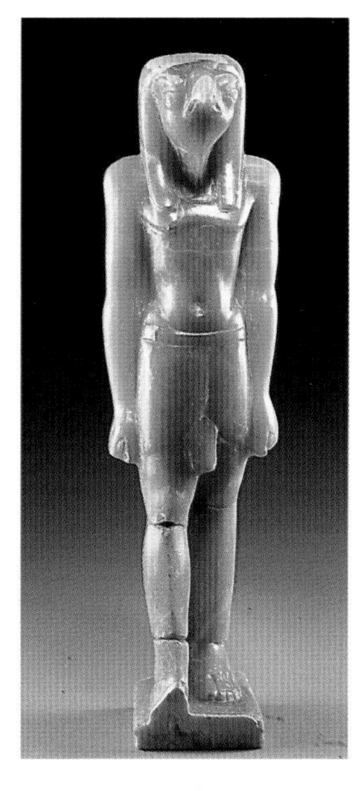

STATUETTE OF HORUS FALCO FROM POMPEII

The statuette, which was discovered in the Pompeiian home of the Amorini Dorati in a sacellum of the peristyle dedicated to the Egyptian triad of Isis, Serapis and Arpocrates, depicts a god-child born from the union between Isis and Osiris resurrected, who was destined to avenge the murder of his father by the cruel Seth, Osiris' brother. Horus Falco, natural heir to the paternal throne, is also a divinity associated with the sun and, therefore, the divine transposition of the image of the Pharaoh.

STATUE OF ANUBIS FROM CUMAE

Long thought to have been found in Pozzuoli, it was discovered in Cumae during the first half of the 19th century together with a mutilated statue of a young boy, which has since been lost, probably depicting Arpocrates (Horus as a child). The statue, which can be dated to the early Imperial period, restores the image of the Egyptian deity Anubis as having human features with a jackal's head, guardian of the dead in Pharaonic Egypt, worthy of having assisted Isis in the search for her dead husband and in looking after the remains of Osiris.

Places dedicated to the cult of isis in the Phlegrean Fields

The discovery in Pozzuoli of cult sites dedicated to oriental and Egyptian divinities was not surprising if one considers the cosmopolitan nature of this harbour centre, truly a terminus for the trade of goods and men ever since the beginning of the 2nd century B.C. The existence of a temple in Pozzuoli dedicated to the god Serapis in the year 105 B.C., has been confirmed by a reference made to it in the *lex parieti faciendo* (a sort of codex of the regulations for the construction of a wall) displayed in the Epigraphic collection of the Museum. The existence of the Iseo (temple of Isis) is confirmed by the inscription of a glass flask from Pozzuoli of a later period. Lastly, the recent discovery of an inscribed altar indicates the presence of a sanctuary to the Nabataean god Dusares in the harbour area where the statue of Isis Pelagia sculpted in grey marble, and a fragment of a naos (small temple), today housed in the Archaeological Museum of Naples, once may have belonged. The recent discovery on the beach of Cumae of a sanctuary to Isis, has brought to light a basalt statuette of the goddess, a sphinx and a naophoros with an image of Osiris. These pieces will enrich the Egyptian Collection of the Neapolitan Museum.

Statue of Isis

Roman Sculpture in Campania

This section, which is located in the west wing on the ground floor (Rooms 30-45), will house sculptures and inscriptions of the Roman period discovered in the cities of Campania, especially Pompeii, Herculaneum, Cumae, and the Phlegrean area. It will also house statues and other monuments which are currently displayed in the atrium of the Museum, or kept in the storage rooms. Due both to their fame and importance, mention must be made of the decorative complex of the Theatre and the Basilica of Herculaneum, the honorary statues of Pompeii, the cult images of the *Capitolium* of Cumae, and the sculptural furnishings of the Imperial Palace of Baia and the Phlegrean villas.

Statue of Eumachia, from Pompeii

Statue of Marcus Holconius Rufus

The statue was dedicated during the Augustan period to one of the most noted citizens of Pompeii, Marcus Holconius Rufus, whose fame derived more from the construction of a public theatre than from his virtues in the military field. It was situated in the heart of Pompeii under a quadrifrontal arch, at the cross-roads between Via Stabiana and Via dell'Abbondanza. In spite of Rufus' fame, he chose to be represented with his armour and cloak, following a model derived from the simulacrum of Mars Ultor (Mars the Avenger) in the temple dedicated to him in the Augustan Forum in Rome. The inscription found under the statue recalls the political career of this man, who vaunts a military tribuneship, the priesthood of the imperial cult, the duumvir, and lastly the title of Patron of the colony of Pompeii.

Statue of Tiberius Pontifex Maximus

This statue, which was found in 1741 during the excavations sponsored by the Bourbons in the area of the theatre of Herculaneum, represents the Emperor Tiberius as pontifex maximus wearing a toga and with a veil over his head; he is portrayed in a pose which closely recalls the better known marble statue of Augustus in Via Labicana and which reflects the programme of scrupulous restoration marked by the importance of the *pietas* and the ancestral traditions inaugurated by the prince at the beginning of a new era.

Statue of Eumachia

The statue depicts the famous Pompeian priestess after whom the monumental complex facing the civic forum was named, dedicated to the *Concordia* and to the *Pietas Augusta* and used for the imperial cult and the *publica magnificentia*, according to a model inaugurated in Rome by the Porticus Liviae on the Esquiline. It was donated by the weavers and dyers of Pompeii as a sign of gratitude and appreciation to their benefactress. It is characterised by the pure classical style of the period; the stance, the veiled head, and the facial features reveal the ideal transfiguration with which Augustan sculpture chose to symbolise *pietas* and moral nobility.

Portrait of Lucius Caecilius Iucundus

The portrait was discovered in the atrium of the Pompeian home of Lucius Caecilius Iucundus, well-known for his activity as a banker and a businessman, due to the discovery of a large archive of wax tablets. The bronze portrait placed on an inscribed marble pillar (with a dedication by a libertus or freed slave to the genius domus of the master of the house), probably represents an ancestor of his. It dates back to the Augustan period, as is revealed by several facial features such as the protruding ears and the wart on his left cheek, traits which were still tied to the realistic tradition of late Republican Roman portraits.

Statues of one of the Dioscuri

The statue was discovered in one of the buildings of the Imperial Palace of Baia (The Temple of Venus) and it restores the image of one of the most famous Greek twins, Castor the mortal and Pollux the immortal, the first born from the union between Leda and Zeus, while the second was the son of Leda and Tyndareus destined to live on alternate days in the kingdoms of Hades and Olympus, symbols of the two hemispheres (the Earth and the Sky) and the harmony of the universe. The characteristic pointed headgear and the arrangement of the cloak, placed on the left shoulder and falling along the arm on the same side, re-evoke the scheme of the Pompeian artwork from the House of the Dioscuri and probably derive from the sculptural model dedicated by Tiberius on the occasion of the reconstruction of the temple of the Forum in Rome. The statue of Baia, which dates back to the mid 2nd century A.D., holds a sword with his left arm and the horse's reins with his right, the horse being reduced only to the head according to an iconography seen in other works of the Roman period (Cyrene, Leptis Magna, Louvre). More recently, a twin statue has been found in Baia near the Baths, unfortunately in a poorer state of conservation than the first.

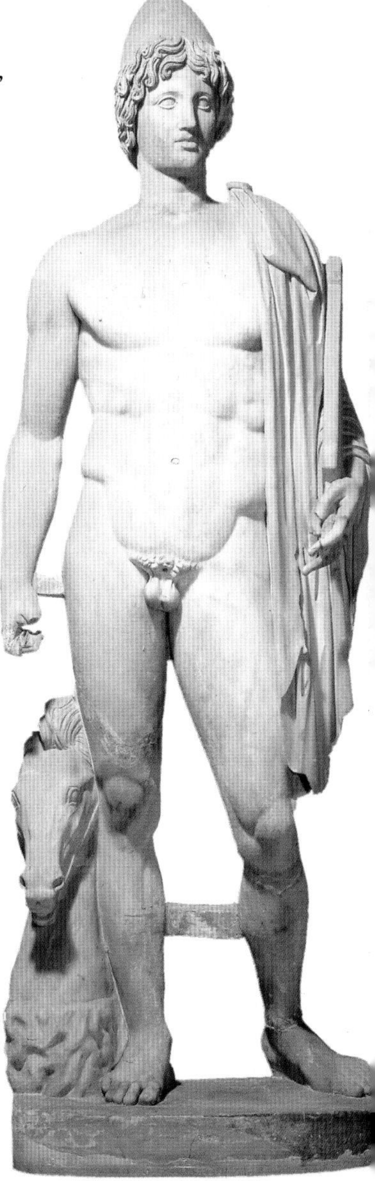

Aphrodite of Capua

The statue, which was initially intended to decorate the portico of the *summa cavea* of the amphitheatre of Capua, is a Hadrianic re-working of a famous Greek model from the late Classical period, representing the goddess of beauty and love looking at her reflection in the shield of her beloved Ares. The style is similar to the Venus-Victoria of Brescia dating to the Augustan period, initially intended to represent Venus the Conqueress, founder of the imperial family, as she writes the epic exploits of the Julians on Mars' shield, and later transformed into Victoria Caesaris by the addition of wings.

Honorary statues and portraits in Rome and in the Roman world

While the Greeks adopted the model of a statue depicting heroic nudity to celebrate the supernatural virtues of their sovereigns and their military heroes, the typical honorary statue of the Roman Republic was a togaed one, used with both religious connotations (augur, pontiff) and military ones (victorions generals).
The Senate had explicitly prohibited, at least initially, the public use of equestrian or loricated statues (Statues depieted wearing armour) even though commonly seen in the Hellenistic milieu, as is clear from the private dedication by Quintus Fabius Maximus, on his return from the victory at Tarentum, who wanted to dedicate an equestrian statue of himself in the Capitol next to the colossal Hercules of Lysippus stolen from the conquered city. However, the profound transformations of the customs that characterised Roman society at the time of the great Asian wars were not long in producing results, as can be seen from the innovative styles widely used in Rome during the Caesarean period. Most notable was the custom of dedicating to local dignitaries both buildings and, in the main squares, nude or military statues, as recalled by Pliny the Elder "at one time statues would be dedicated in togaed attire. Nude statues holding a pole similar to that of the ephebi were well liked: they were placed in the gymnasia and called Achillee. The Greek custom called for not covering anything; whereas the Roman custom was to put on armour…(As well) equestrian statues are highly considered in Rome: without a doubt the example came from Greece" (*Natural History*, 34, 10).
Far removed from the inspiring Greek models were the individual portraits of a realistic type, which corresponded more closely Roman mentality and to the prevailing spirit of the time, characterised by bitter struggles for power and the ambitious triumphalist ideologies of the *homines novi* or "new men".

Equestrian statue of Marcus Nonius Balbus, from Herculaneum

The Greek Masters

The museum is still organised according to the display criteria established at the beginning of the century by the historian Ettore Pais, in line with the canons of the great German archaeological school of the 1800s. The rooms dedicated to the Greek masters contain mainly copies of Greek originals from the Classical period reproduced during the age of Roman Imperialism. Among these is the Athenian group of the Tyrannicides, the Aphrodite Sosandra and the Apollo of the *omphalos* of Kalamis, the Doryphoros of Polycleitus, the Athena, the Hera, and the Nemesis of Agorakritos. There are very few surviving original pieces, two of these being the magnificent statue of Nereid on a pistris (mythological fish) (from a villa in Formia) and an Attic relief representing sacred scenes linked to the mystery of Eleusis found in a villa in the ancient territory of Sinuessa (known today as Mondragone).

Statue of Nereid on a pistris (mythological fish), from Formia

The Tyrannicides

This best preserved Roman copy of the bronze sculptural group known as the Tyrannicides, the work of Antenor, comes from the Villa Adriana in Tivoli. The original was dedicated in 510 B.C. to the memory of Harmodios and Aristogeiton, the young men who had paid with their lives for killing Ipparcus, the son of the tyrant Peisistratos, giving the people of Athens back their freedom. The statues were confiscated by the Persians after Athens was defeated and substituted in 477 B.C. with a new group which was the work of Kritios and Nesiotes. A number of copies of this work are seen especially on reliefs, coins and painted vases.
The head of Aristogeiton was made from a plaster cast of a head housed in the Vatican Museums. An original ancient cast made directly from the original bronze of the Classical era is preserved in the Museum of the Phlegrean Fields in the Castle of Baia.
This sculptural group was already famous in ancient times for having introduced the style of iconic statues, hitherto unknown. In Greece, as recalled by Pliny, "there was the habit of representing only those men who deserved immortality for some illustrious reason; at first for the victories achieved at the sacred games, especially at Olympus, where it was common practice to dedicate a statue to all those who had won, whereas for those who won three times, the statues dedicated to them represented their genitalia in their actual size: they were called iconic. I do not know if the Athenians were the first to erect a statue at the State's expense, and this was in honour of the tyrannicides Harmodios and Aristogeiton...This practice was then welcomed by the entire world" (*Natural History*, 34, 9-10).

Statue of Doryphoros

This is one of the best preserved copies of the original bronze made during the classical period attributed to Polycleitus (440 B.C.). The statue was known in antiquity as *Kanon*, symbolising those principles of harmony and proportion which the sculptor himself had elaborated in a written work known by that name. The figure of the young spearman, once thought to be Achilles, perfectly embodied the athletic and military ideals of the ruling classes of Athens during that period.
The statue was found in the Samnite Palestra of Pompeii among the sculptural ornaments which were part of the reconstruction of the complex carried out during the Augustan Age. This period saw the revival of works of the Classical period, especially those by Polycleitus, thus assuring the achievement of perfection in representing the human form.

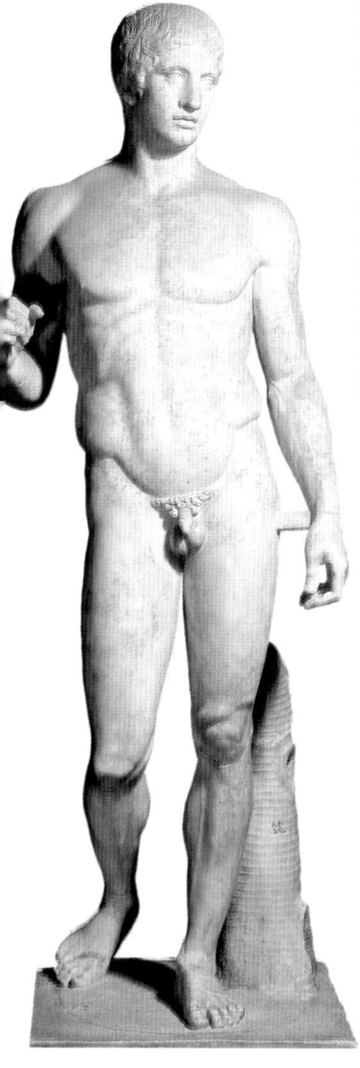

Artemis from Pompeii

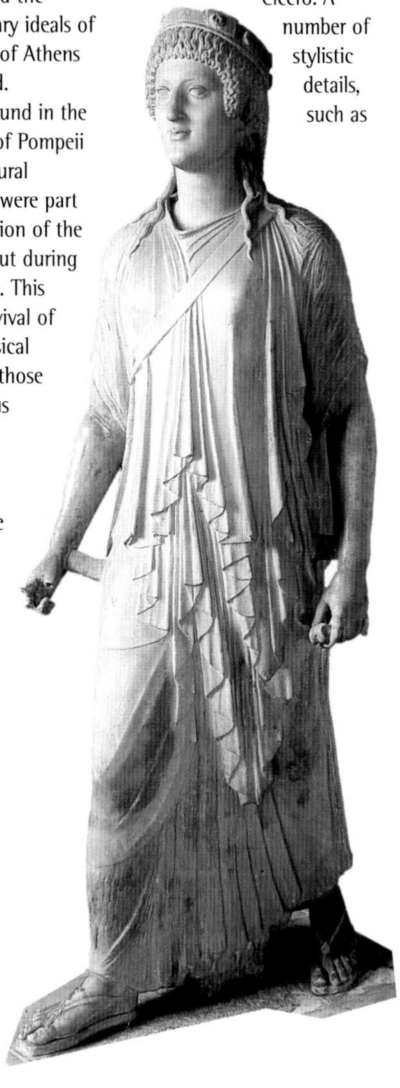

This Pentelic marble sculpture is a Roman copy from the late Republican period of a Greek original from archaic times, perhaps the Diana of Segesta as recalled by Cicero. A number of stylistic details, such as

the smoothness of the marble surface and the softness of the drapings, lead us to attribute the work to the Neo-Attic studio of Pasiteles, who worked during the 1st century B.C. The revival of archaic forms is a recurrent phenomenon in ancient sculpture from the Classical period right through to the age of Imperialism, and guaranteed both the artists and their works an aura of unmatchable solemnity and sacredness, in the same way as the use of rhetorical speech where the adoption of "archaising" expressions lent a "grandiose" effect to a speech (Quintilianus, VIII, 3, 24 s.).

Relief representing Dionysus visiting *Ikaria*

This relief, at one time part of the Borgia Collection, is one of many surviving copies. It represents an inebriated Dionysus visiting the home of one of his followers. He is held up by a small satyr and is followed by an orgiastic procession. To the left, the master of the house is lying down on a triclinial bed with a woman and raising his right arm as a sign of welcome.
It would have originally adorned the walls of a wealthy Roman house. It is dated to the late Republican period and can be included in the prolific iconographic production dedicated to Dionysus and his colourful world; this subject enjoyed considerable popularity during the period dominated by the conflict between Octavius, follower of the teachings of Apollo, and Mark Antony, who was celebrated as the new Dionysus of the Orient.

The Farnese Collection

This extraordinary collection of antiquities begun by Pope Paul III Farnese and continued by his nephew Cardinal Alexander (over 400 sculptures are included in Domenico Venuti's inventory, as well as paintings, gems, books and drawings), adorned the Roman estates of this noble family during the 17th century, and especially the grand building which now houses the French Embassy. Other works which were considered of minor importance were kept in the remaining Roman residences (Villa Madama, Villa Farnesina at Lungara, and the Farnese Gardens on the Palatine Hills), in the Villa Caprarola and in the Ducal Palace of Colorno in Parma (the latter can boast the possession at one time of the two basalt *colossi* of Hercules and Dionysius excavated by Abbot Bianchini in Rome near the Imperial Palace). The statues, which were discovered in the Roman complex of the Baths of Caracalla, are still today a symbol of the preciousness and richness of the collection. Among these, the Farnese Bull is a masterpiece of ancient art which shares with the Laocoonte of the Vatican Museums the privilege of being mentioned in the Natural History of Pliny the Elder.
The transfer of the Farnese family to Parma reduced the fame of the Roman collection, which was later inherited by the Bourbons (1731) through Elisabetta, the wife of Philip V of Spain and mother of Charles, King of Naples (1734). It was Charles' successor Ferdinand IV who created the Royal Bourbonic Museum and transferred the prestigious Farnese collection to Naples, where it has remained ever since as the noble and vital heart of the Museum.

The Farnese Bull

This colossal marble sculptural group represents the myth of Dirce (she was tied to a wild bull by the sons of Antiope, Zeto and Amphion, who wanted to punish her for the ill-treatment inflicted on their mother, first wife of Lykos, King of Thebes). It was discovered in 1545 near the Baths of Caracalla during the excavations commissioned by Pope Paul III Farnese in the hope of finding ancient sculptures to adorn his Roman residence. The writings of Pliny on this work inform us of the names of the sculptors, Apollonios and Tauriskos, as well as their artistic environment, namely the Rhodian school of the end of the 2nd century B.C. The reaction of artists and intellectuals to the discovery of this work of art was truly extraordinary. In many ways it was quite similar to the reaction a few years earlier when the Laocoon was discovered, causing many to describe “this marvellous mountain of marble as the most singular and marvellous work of the chisel of the ancient world, and which the art of sculpting can achieve in its most excellent form”. It was shipped to Naples in 1788, where it arrived escorted by a war ship, and was placed in the garden of the royal villa as the central ornament of a fountain. In 1826 it was brought to the National Museum to be permanently displayed there.

The Farnese Bull in the Collection of Asinius Pollio

Pliny the Elder (*Natural History*, 36, 34) recalls that the sculptural group representing Zeto, Amphion, Dirce and the Bull (sculpted, along with the cord that ties them together, from one block of marble) is the work of Apollonios and Tauriskos. Imported from Rhodes, it was part of the magnificent collection of artwork owned by Asinius Pollio, a Roman politician who lived during the years between the Republic and the Princedom. He created the first public library in Rome containing works by Greek and Latin authors, adorned by the images of famous literary men (the only one who had the honour of being portrayed while still alive was Terence), later imitated by Octavian with the Palatine library in the Sanctuary of Apollo. Linked to the library was the precious collection of works of art, especially the Hellenistic ones which Asinius Pollio preferred above anything else in the world, and which Pliny recalls as consisting of statues of satyrs and maenads, Dionysus and Naiad (Pliny, *Natural History*, 36, 33). Asinius Pollio's decision to open up to the public the art treasures of his home (the library and art collection) was incredibly innovative for the period.

Farnese Hercules

This colossal statue was discovered during the mid-1500s near the Baths of Caracalla and was displayed in the courtyard of Palazzo Farnese in Rome until 1787. From there it was moved to Naples, first to Capodimonte and then, in 1792, to the newly opened museum in the Palazzo degli Studi. During the hectic years of French rule, the statue was prevented from being shipped to France by Napoleon at least three times. It has been restored on numerous occasions but the most famous restoration was that carried out by Guglielmo della Porta commissioned by Michelangelo. Della Porta remade the lost legs of the statue and when the original legs were found, the Farnese family refused to have them substituted "in order to demonstrate that works of modern sculpture could be compared to ancient works". The original legs were re-inserted by the Bourbons after the King of Naples received them as a gift from the Borghese family. The carved inscription identifies the sculptor as the Athenian Glicone. It is a copy of the bronze "Hercules at rest" by Lysippus.

Ephesian Artemis

This cult simulacrum from one of the main sanctuaries of the eastern Greek world is best known for its iconography, passed on to us by means of the coins minted in Ephesos during the Hellenistic age. The features which characterise the figure are: the *kalathos* worn by the goddess on her head, the circular nimbus decorated with the heads of griffins, the row of breasts (or the scrota of bulls which had been sacrificed) on her chest symbolising the vital and regenerative strength of the goddess, and lastly, the heads of animals, sphinxes and bees found on the lower part of her clothing. This exemplar from the Farnese Collection is a copy made in precious alabaster during the Imperial age. The parts in bronze date back to the restoration by Giuseppe Valadier.

The Farnese Gems

The collection of gems was bequeathed to Charles III by the last Duke of Parma, and then transferred to Naples in 1735 to be displayed at the Royal Villa of Capodimonte. The original Collection, which dates back to Ranuccio and Alessandro Farnese, heirs to Paul III, was later enriched by the remarkable collection of Fulvio Orsini, the learned humanist patronised by the Farnese family, and by several exemplars belonging to the de'Medici family which were brought by Margherita of Austria, mother of Alessandro Farnese, as a dowry. Between the end of the 1500s and the beginning of the 1600s there were just over 500 gems in the Collection, some of which ended up in Northern European collections in mysterious circumstances. Little is known regarding the origins and the dates of acquisition of the other gems, both ancient and more modern, which make up the present-day collection.

The Farnese Cup

This is a unique example of the glyptics of the Hellenistic era, both in terms of its dimensions as well as its magnificence. The Farnese Cup was made at the Egyptian Ptolemaic Court and from there was transferred to Rome after the victory of Octavius over Cleopatra. In fact, it is the religiosity of the Alexandrian world, so rich in symbols, with which the Cup can be identified: the goddess Isis sitting on a sphinx and holding a sheaf of wheat in her hand; Osiris-Serapis holding the horn of plenty; the young Horos-Harpokrates with a plough and a bag of seeds; all surrounded by the personifications of the Seasons (or the Aurora and the Morning Dew) and the Etesian Winds. The Egyptian triad, which was already compared to the Eleusinian mysteries regarding Demeter, Dionysus and the young Triptolemus, was a clear allusion to the reigning Lagidi family, symbolised near the end of the 2nd century B.C., represented by Cleopatra III, Ptolemy VIII and the young Ptolemy X Alexander. The high quality of the workmanship of the Farnese Cup has represented, since ancient times, the pride of court treasures from the court of Ptolemies, the Roman Imperial court, the Byzantine court, the court of Frederick II, the Persian court, the Aragonese court, and then, more recently from the Medici to the Farnese family.

Artemis, signed by Apollonios, engraved amethyst

Bust of a Moor, cameo in sardonyx agate

Competition between Athena and Poseidon for the control of Attica, inscribed Lau.r.med, cameo in sardonyx agate

Hippolytus, a hunt companion, Phaedra and the wet-nurse, inscribed Lau.r.med, cameo in sardonyx agate

Orpheus playing, cameo in brecciated agate

Icarus and Daedalus, Pasiphae and Artemis, inscribed Lau.r.med, cameo in sardonyx agate

Tiberius, cameo in lapis lazuli

Nike on a chariot, inscribed Lau.r.med, signed by Sostratos, cameo in sardonyx agate

Apollo, Olympus and Marsyas (the so-called Nero's seal), inscribed Lau.r.med, engraved in cornelian

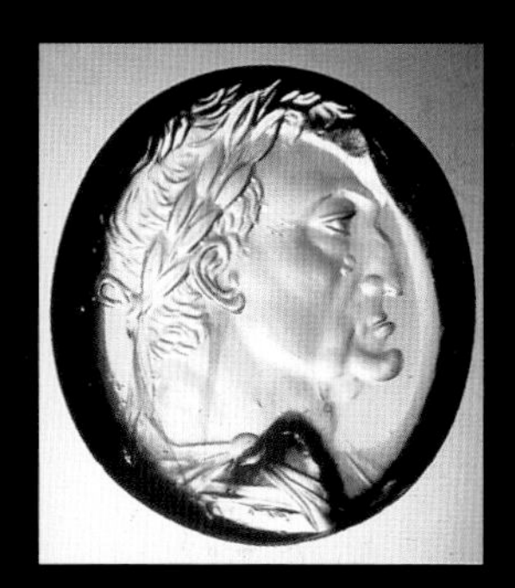

The Carracci Gallery

This was the name of one of the most famous rooms of Palazzo Farnese in Rome. It was built by Cardinal Odoardo, and the frescoes were painted by the Bolognese artist Annibale Carracci at the end of the 16th century. The Gallery was designed with ten niches and six *tondi* and housed antique statues and busts. The statues, which are now divided between the Museum of Naples and the British Museum of London, included such works as Dionysus, Eros, Apollo, Hermes, and Antinous, the statue of Ceres and the sculptural groups representing Ganymede embracing Zeus' eagle, and the Satyr with Dionysus as a child.

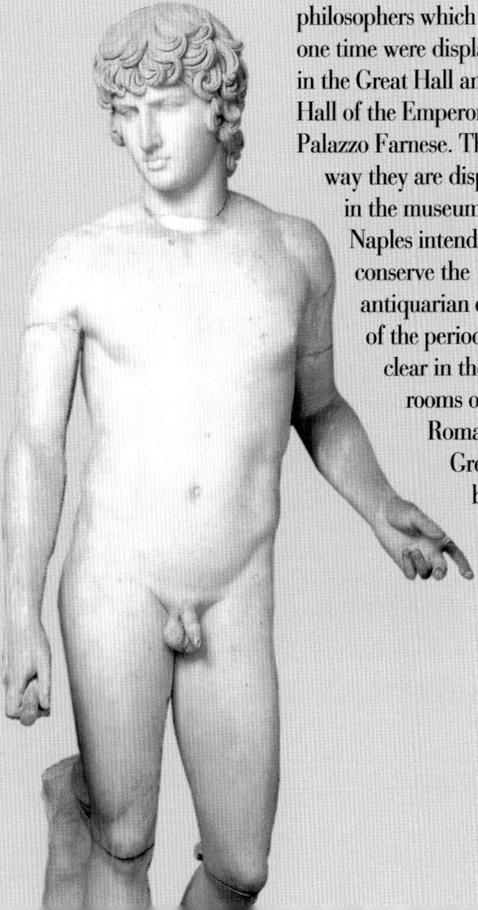

hermae of Greek intellectuals and philosophers which at one time were displayed in the Great Hall and the Hall of the Emperors at Palazzo Farnese. The way they are displayed in the museum of Naples intends to conserve the antiquarian ethos of the period, as is clear in the two rooms of Roman and Greek busts.

Farnese Caracalla

The bust of the Emperor Caracalla was already mentioned in the 1568 inventory of the Farnese Collection. It adorned the Roman Palace of the family until it was transferred to Naples in 1796 (first to Capodimonte, then to the Palazzo degli Studi). The fame of this work during the 1600s and 1700s is linked to the Roman Emperor's bad reputation caused by his violent temper and the responsibility for fratricide which led Winckelmann to write that Lysippus could not have made a better portrait. A bronze copy was commissioned by Pope Pius IV from Guglielmo della Porta for his Vatican Belvedere Collection; it later became part of the Roman Farnese Collection and is today housed in the Museum of Capodimonte.

Bust of Homer

The facial features of the greatest Greek poet had been reproduced since classical times, starting a tradition which continued until the end of the Empire. The distinctive elements of his portrait were his blindness and old age, the first one being almost an essential condition for the memory, and the second one being a natural condition for whoever practises the art of the scholar and intellectual. As testified by the words of Kristodoros at the sight of the statue of the poet at the Baths of Constantinople: "...the features of an old man, but of a gentle old age, so much so that it gives him an even richer aura of grace: a mixture of venerability and dearness, from which prestige glimmered through... With his two hands, one on top of the other asking for support from his staff, as one does among the living. The right ear bent, always seeming to listen to Apollo, almost as if he could hear a Muse nearby..." (*Anthologia Palatina*, II, 311-349).

Herm of Socrates

The appearance of the philosopher is well-known from the description of Xenophon who referred to his protruding eyes, snub nose with wide nostrils and full lips (*Symposium*, V, 5-7) and that of Plato comparing Socrates to the silenus Marsyas (*Symposium*, 215, 216d), renowned in Greek myths as an educator of heroic or divine children and dispenser of goodness and wisdom. On the pillar of the Farnese herma, in addition to the name of the philosopher in Greek, there is also a passage from Plato's Kriton: "not today for the first time, but I have always been so, that to nothing that belongs to me do I bend my willpower if not to the strength of reasoning that appears to me to be the best", in memory of the last will pronounced by Socrates before being sentenced to death by the people of Athens. The sculptor of this portrait, a copyist of the early Imperial age, was inspired by the model of the statue made by Lysippus and commissioned by Demetrios of Phaleron; as a result of the guilt felt by the people of Athens for having condemned the philosopher to death (Diogene Laerzio, II, 43), it was decided to add a smile to render the facial features of Socrates more humane and to soften the more silenic features.

The Mosaic Collection

Mosaic column from Pompeii, Villa of the Mosaic Columns

Mosaic female portrait, from Pompeii, VI, 15, 4

This collection is among the finest in existence, above all on account of the exceptional preservation from the Vesuvian cities. It has maintained almost in its entirety the nineteenth-century display deriving from a museological approach which tended to separate the various classes of artistic production at the expense of their place of origin. It is scheduled to be renewed by re-uniting the groups into their original entirety.

The Mosaics of Dioskourides

These two small, refined mosaics, which bear the signature of Dioskourides, were found in the so-called Villa of Cicero discovered in Pompeii in 1763 right outside the Gate of Herculaneum, and subsequently re-buried. Influenced by Hellenistic art of the 3rd century B.C., the first mosaic portrays street musicians, whereas the second is inspired by the plot of a play by Menander and depicts the consultation of a sorceress.

The Mosaics of the House of the Faun at Pompeii

These mosaics unquestionably represent the most precious part of the Neapolitan collection, both in terms of the quality and number of subjects, as well as the fame which followed the discovery of the excavation.
The famous bronze statuette of the dancing Faun, from which the traditional name of the house derives (dedicated in the 1800s to Goethe or to the "Gran Musaico" (the Great Mosaic) of Alexander), is a clear and direct reference to the Hellenistic court of Alexandria in Egypt and to its rich iconographic repertoire, full of references to the Dionysian and theatrical sphere. Right from the start, the discovery of the Pompeian Faun was the object of admiration and renown, so much so that an English traveller in 1838 wrote: "it is not the most marvellous statue in the world simply because the Faun is not the most marvellous creature in the world...It is, however, the Venus de'Medici of the Sylvans, begging forgiveness for this change of gender".
The luxurious mosaic panels (*emblemata*), which recall the colourful world of Dionysus and the Greek theatre, adorned a number of rooms in the house: these included the threshold between the entrance vestibule of the house and the Tuscan atrium (emblem with a rich festoon of flowers and fruit adorned by two tragic female masks with long curly wigs); a room next to the atrium (a double emblem depicting a cat capturing a partridge and Nilotic ducks with lotus flowers in their beaks); banquet halls (an emblem depicting Dionysus as a child riding a tiger in the centre of a vegetable frame with theatrical masks, and an emblem depicting marine fauna centring on a lobster capturing a squid), and a bedroom (an erotic emblem depicting Satyr and Nymph).
The large mosaic of the threshold of the exedra depicts an exotic Nilotic scene filled with ducks, snakes, crocodiles and hippopotamuses. This scene is an introduction to the main decoration of the hall, which is centred around the celebration of Alexander and the founding of Alexandria. It is made up of a monumental mosaic depicting the battle which assured Alexander's conquest of Asia, and his arrival at the rich Delta region, a scene already captured in paintings by a great artist of Early Hellenism, Philoxenes of Eretria, mentioned by Pliny the Elder (*Natural History*, 35, 110).
The rich mosaic decorations of the House of the Faun are the work of skilled Alexandrian craftsmen, active in Italy between the end of the 2nd century B.C. and the beginning of the following century, the period during which the imposing restructuring of the Pompeian "palace" took place; its size and sumptuousness evoked the *fasti* (the magnificence) of the oriental Hellenistic palaces.
The chronology of the Pompeian mosaics follows the writings of Pliny the Elder when he refers to the custom of inserting medallions in the centre of the flooring, which were executed separately (*emblemata*) and made of tiny coloured tesserae, a custom already documented in Rome during the second half of the 2nd century B.C. (*Natural History*, 36, 61).

Threshold with theatrical masks and festoon with fruit and flowers

Emblem depicting a cat capturing a partridge and Nilotic ducks

Threshold with a Nilotic scene

Emblem with Dionysus as a child riding a tiger

Monumental mosaic depicting the battle of Alexander the Great

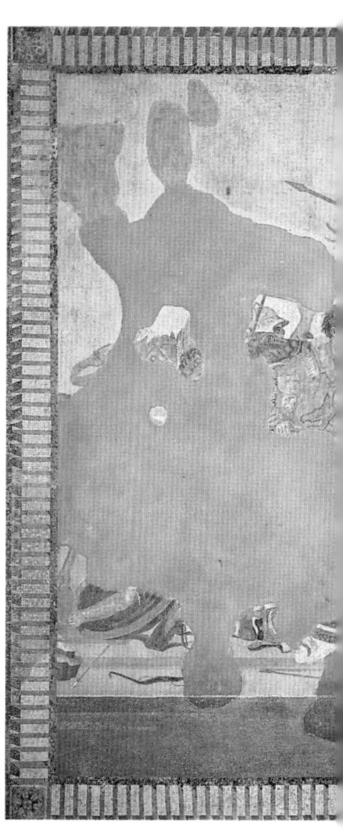

Emblem depicting marine fauna

Emblem depicting doves on a jewellery-box

Mosaic depicting a crater and doves

"The most famous craftsman of mosaic floors was Sosos, who built a floor in Pergamum known as the *asaraton oecon*, because he used small multi-coloured tesserae to depict table scraps and other bits of rubbish which are usually swept away as if they had just been left there; there is a splendid dove drinking whose head casts a shadow over the water, while the other birds enjoy the sunlight as they scratch themselves on the edge of a cantharus" (Pliny, *Natural History*, 36, 60).

A number of copies of the work of art from Pergamum, mentioned by Pliny, were known both in Rome and the Roman world. Among these is the mosaic with the doves from Santa Maria Capua Vetere, dating back to the end of the 1st century B.C.

The Secret Room

Rattle in the form of a gladiator, from Herculaneum

The embarrassment of the excavators at the archaeological sites of Pompeii and Herculaneum during the Bourbonic era, caused by finding evidence of explicit erotica, finds an echo in contemporary documents (comparing Pompeii to the legendary Sodom) and in the decision made to reserve a "closed" room for the display of these artefacts in the Herculanean Museum of Portici, accessible only to those few who managed to obtain a special permit from the Court functionaries. The more liberal approach of those behind the new museum at Palazzo degli Studi, who decided to display the "secret" collection to the public, was soon curbed by an upsurge of moralism due to a visit to the Museum by the daughter of Francis I. It was for this reason that a specific "Private Room of Obscene Objects" was created and opened only to those "persons of a mature age and a well-known morality". At the time, the collection contained 102 objects which were "infamous monuments of heathen licentiousness". During the years of the revolution, those requesting more leniency in granting permission to see the exhibition, were opposed by others who wanted to prevent even the exhibition of the nude or semi-nude Venuses in the Museum of Naples. As often happens, the reactionary spirit had its way and the exhibition was hidden away on the first floor and forgotten by most. Since then, the Secret Room has gone through various phases according to the political circumstances of the time: it was opened during Garibaldi's arrival in Naples and semi-closed during the Savoy government and the Fascist régime up until 1967. The work currently underway will soon return the exhibition to the public, with the exception of the younger visitors to the Museum.

Marble group representing Pan and a Goat

A refined and sophisticated evocation of the wild and savage world of Pan, the rustic god of the woods, represented as a man with a goat's legs, horns and ears, comparable to the Roman Faun. This marble group was found in 1752 among other ornaments of the garden of the Villa of the Papyri in Herculaneum. It is a copy of an original Greek statue from the mid-Hellenistic period.

Mosaic representing a Satyr and a Nymph from the House of the Faun

This vermicular mosaic emblem (which was destined for the intimacy of the bedroom and is made of polychromatic *tesserae* which are so tiny and sparkling as to evoke the image of swarming worms, *vermes* in Latin), represents an amorous encounter between a Satyr and a Nymph. It is quite similar to another exemplar discovered near the Nile delta, thus leaving little doubt as to the origins of the craftsmen commissioned to decorate this noble Pompeian home.

The Numismatic Collection

Gold medallion of Augustus, from Pompeii

The Museum has a magnificent collection of over 200,000 pieces originating from both the initial Farnese Collection patiently put together by the humanist Fulvio Orsini as part of his studies on antique iconography and Imperial portraiture, as well as from the excavations in the Vesuvian cities, promoted during the Bourbonic age. Apart from the rich discoveries, including antique coins, made in those years of early archaeology, there were also private coin collections, such as the Santangelo Collection acquired by the Museum of Naples in 1864. The first exhibition room (Room 51) is dedicated to the history of numismatics and the analysis of coin collecting by means of a small but important selection from the Museum's private collections. The second exhibition room (Room 52) contains coins from some of the most important Greek colonies in southern Italy and in Sicily (Sybaris, Tarentum, Rhegium, Zancle), which document the different monetary systems adopted: the Achaean one (based on the Corinthian tri-dram weighing 8 grams) and the Chaldaean one (based on a dram weighing 5.70 grams). The third exhibition room (Room 53) illustrates the monetary system of Campania, ranging from the first issues from Cumae to the well-known series coined by Neapolis. A special section is devoted to the coins of Sicily, ranging from the most antique pieces from Selinunte, Agrigento and Gela which date back to the second half of the 6th century B.C., to more recent ones coined in Syracuse by the tyrant Dionysius I which have a bronze core and an elegantly engraved gold or silver exterior. The collection of Italic coins conserved in the Museum of Naples is just as noteworthy, from the primitive *aes rude* (unrefined metal used for exchange) and to Republican coins (the as and its denominations) and Augustan currency, including the brass *sestertii* and *dupondii*, and the copper *as* and its denominations *quadrantes*. Together with the antique coin exhibition, there are also numerous illustrated documents (paintings and sculptures), which are useful for reconstructing the society and economy of the Vesuvian cities, such as the marble relief depicting scenes from a coppersmith's shop, or the paintings depicting everyday scenes such as the sale of bread, cooked food or work utensils. Exhibition Room 55 contains documents of the Middle Ages found in Campania and Sicily, and concludes with the monetary history of the Two Sicilies from Norman times up to the Bourbon dynasty.

1 *Beaten stater with the Ami inscription, from Cittanova*

2 *Di-dram of Cora*

3 *Beaten stater from Caulonia*

4 *Deca-dram from Syracuse*

5 *Di-dram from Allifae*

6 *Denarius of Brutus*

The Great Hall of the Sundial

The statue known as the Farnese Atlante, which represents one of the most detailed and precise ancient representations of the Zodiac, was most certainly conceived in the fertile scientific environment of the Court of Alexandria. The interest surrounding the statue was certainly known to whoever decided in 1791 to place it in the Great Hall of the Palazzo degli Studi in Naples, and then had to be satisfied with making a sundial which is still in use today due to the ray of light which enters the room through a hole made in the south-west upper corner.
The paintings which adorn the upper part of the walls are from the Genoese School and are dedicated to the noble deeds of Alessandro Farnese, general of Charles V. They were once displayed together with the tapestries representing the victory of the Farnese in the Battle of Pavia (now in the Museum of Capodimonte). The frescoes on the vaulted ceiling of the room are the work of Piero Bardellino, and illustrate the artistic accomplishments of Ferdinand IV and his wife.

The decorative arts and furnishings of the homes of Pompeii

The archaeological excavations of the Vesuvian cities represented in the past, and still do today, an extraordinary source of knowledge of all aspects of social and everyday life of Republican and Imperial Rome, as is documented by the architecture of the houses, the floor and wall decorations, the furnishings and other household items.
A magnificent array of household furnishings are on display in the east wing of the first floor, including precious silver accessories, fine ceramic tableware, personal ornaments, gladiatorial equipment, glass vases, small and large bronze decorative sculptures, kitchen utensils and table settings, and clay lares.

Silver mirror from Pompeii

The Hellenisation of Roman lifestyles, and the advent of *Asian luxuria* in Roman houses of the Republic had a great influence on the architectural transformations of the classical home with an atrium, by bringing innovations such as "high regal vestibules, wide atriums and peristyles, extremely large gardens and porticoes, as well as libraries, picture galleries and basilicas which were as magnificent as the public ones" (Vitruvius, VI,5,2). The decorative arts and tableware were also influenced: the simple and decorous household items of ancient times were substituted by refined and precious silver table services which the nobles loved to flaunt at their feasts and banquets as a sign of their social and economic status.

Antique pieces were particularly sought after, such as the cups depicting bucolic scenes found among the treasures of the House of Menander, or the bronze *hydria* from the Classical epoch used as a fountain in the Pompeian home of Julius Polibius.
The decorative designs of the furnishings of the triclinium and the living room were inspired by the Greek myths, and the sculptures placed as ornaments in the homes and gardens were copied from Classical and Hellenistic age prototypes. An oil-lamp holder statue found in the Pompeian home of the Citharist is said to have been inspired by an Apollo by the master of Phidias, and was considered to be a perfect example of the fashion so criticised by contemporary moralists of using "gold statues of young men holding a lit torch with their right hand in order to illuminate the nocturnal orgies" (Lucretius, *The Nature of Things*, II, 20s).
The coming of Empire introduced new figurative themes, all of which responded to the commemorative ideology of the emperor and his gens, and spread to both the public and private spheres of life. For example, even the intimacy of the family lararium was affected, as seen by the terracotta group representing Aeneas escaping from Troy with the old Anchises and the young Ascanius, chosen by Augustus as the official symbol of the Trojan origins of the Julian gens, and here used as a sign of private devotion to the designs and figures of the official religion.

Obsidian cups from Stabia

Silverware from the House of Menander

The House of Menander, so-called because of the painted panel depicting the Greek playwright, is the source of a magnificent silverware treasure, today displayed in the Museum of Naples. It is made up of 118 pieces, several of which are quite ancient and evidently restored. The vases were kept on the bottom of a wooden case, placed in the cellar during the reconstruction of the house after the earthquake in A.D. 62, and covered by pieces of cloth and wool. The upper part of the case contained the family jewels (earrings, necklaces, gold bracelets and rings set with precious stones), and a hoard of gold and silver coins amounting to 1,432 *sestertii.*

Among the silverware were several valuable cups embossed with scenes of the myths (the love of Mars and Venus; the labours of Hercules; Dionysus and his entourage), or with traditional Hellenistic landscapes, often the work of the Greek *argentarius* silversmith Apelles. The owner of this luxurious home, or at least the last owner, is thought to be Quintus Poppeo, a well-known tile-maker related to Poppaea Augustus, the second wife of Nero, who owned the Villa of Oplontis.

The Blue glass vase

This vase was supposedly discovered in a tomb of the Pompeian cemetery at the Gate of Herculaneum, at whose opening King Ferdinand II was present. It is made of cameo glassware using a special technique which involves the application of a layer of white vitreous paste to parts of a blue glass base which was omitted where the blue background was desired. In this case, the scene represented is the Dionysian theme of grape-harvesting. The scene, which is surrounded by Dionysian masks from which grapevines intertwine populated by birds, includes the joyous figures of cupids who are either pressing grapes, banqueting or playing the flute and the syrinx.
The same technique was used for the two panels representing Dionysian scenes which were probably part of the decoration of a triclinium of furniture from the Pompeian House of Fabius Rufus, now in the Museum of Naples.

Alexander on horseback

The bronze statues from Herculaneum, one portraying Alexander on horseback and another of a riderless horse, are the only known evidence, even though on a smaller scale, of the equestrian monument made by Lysippus in memory of the Macedonian victory over the Persians at the river Granicus (334 B.C.). Lysippus' statue was dedicated by Alexander in the sanctuary of Zeus Olympia in Dione, Macedonia. In particular, this monument was intended as a memorial to the twenty-five noble Macedonians who fell in the first phase of the battle. The statue from Herculaneum portraying Alexander attacking the enemy, reveals the close attention shown to the fine details; the Macedonian king is portrayed fully armed with a chiton, armour and a cloak, and the regal diadem on his head on the horse Bukephalos.
The statue, which was found in Herculaneum in 1761, dates back to the end of the 1st century B.C.

The Sanctuary of Isis in Pompeii

Statue of Isis, from Pompeii

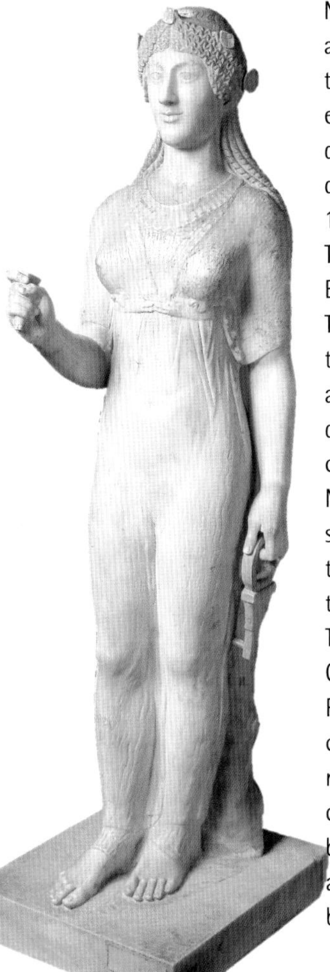

The decision to re-organising the furnishings of the Temple of Isis from Pompeii in Rooms 79-82 of the Museum of Naples, is the result of a new way of conceiving a museum of antiquities, whilst taking care at the same time to maintain the original context of provenance. The success of this endeavour is mainly due to the wealth of contemporary documentation from the time of the building's discovery, during the first years of the Bourbonic excavations (between 1764 and 1766).

The sanctuary was built towards the end of the 2nd century B.C. in the area of the Pompeian Theatres and close to the Temple of Aesculapius and the Temple of Minerva which, for the occasion, had fencing put round it and was adorned by an elegant *tholos* and propylaeum at the entrance. The damage caused by the earthquake of A.D. 62 required the complete reconstruction of the building financed by Numerius Popidius Ampliatus in honour of his six-year-old son Celsinus, as recalled by a dedicatory inscription placed in the main entrance in memory of the occasion, which gave to the boy the honour of free admission to the civic Senate.

The temple was surrounded by a portico which, after Celsinus' reconstruction, assumed the characteristics of "a Rhodian peristyle" as described by Vitruvius, with eight columns on each of the two longer sides, seven on the narrow west end, and six on the narrow east end. This type of construction was well-known in Pompeii, both in private buildings (for example, the House of the Silver Anniversary) and in public ones (Eumachia's Building). The splendid, brightly coloured decoration on the end wall painted in the

Fourth Style has red panels which alternate Isian scenes and small landscapes and architecture. An elegant frieze runs along the top border with gyrals and objects, related to the cult of Isis, on a black background surmounted by small still-life pictures which allude to the sacrifices offered in honour of the goddess.
The actual temple is located in the centre of the courtyard, a tetrastyle prostyle on a high podium, with the exterior and interior walls of the *cella* (cell) completely covered in white stucco in imitation of *opus quadratum* (Roman masonry of squared blocks). Along the back wall there was a brick platform used to hold the cult statues of Isis and Osiris; behind the podium, in a niche, a statue of Dionysus with a panther was found, with a dedication by Numerius Popidius Ampliatus. Two other niches were found on either side of the entrance, which may have contained the statues of Arpocrates and Anubis who also had two altars dedicated to them in the courtyard, in line with the niches. Unfortunately, the mosaic floors of the *cella* (cell) are lost, documented only by the drawings of Piranesi.
There were many altars with dedicatory inscriptions in the courtyard, which also had a small enclosed underground room used for purification ceremonies, and known as the *purgatorium*. The enclosure-wall is richly decorated with paintings and stuccoes which depict the love between Mars and Venus, and Perseus and Andromeda. The east side of the courtyard housed the *ekklesiasterion*, a room used for meetings and banquets as well as the actual *sacrarium*. The painted decorations of this first room are quite noteworthy, such as the famous paintings of the myths of Io arriving in Canopos and the liberation of Argus from captivity. The paintings in the shrine were of less importance, depicting scenes with figures and symbols of the world of Isis.
The architecture of the sanctuary or temple is completed by a complex of three rooms located south-east of the courtyard and known as the *pastophorion* (apartment of the priests), as well as a series of other rooms identified as being a kitchen, a triclinium and a cubicle, decorated with Fourth Style frescoes.

Among the sculptural furnishings was a bronze herm of Norbanus Sorex found in the portico and dating to the early Augustan age, an archaic-style statue of Isis which was a votive offering by Lucius Caecilius Febus and dates to the reign of the emperor Claudius, the head of a goddess found near the entrance to the *ekklesiasterion* and, lastly, two female portraits of early Imperial date. The only evidence of the Samnite phase was a fragmentary puteal terracotta which gives us a rare image of a Dionysian *thiasos* (the god's procession) contemplating the participation of Hercules, together with Dionysus and others with him.

Previous page:
Panels representing priests wearing the ceremonial costume of the "Isis ceremonies"

Painting of Io at Canopos, from the so-called ekklesiasterion

Bronze herma of Caius Norbanus Sorex

The Pompeian temple of Isis

Many authors had already fallen under the spell of the myth of Isis even before the discovery of the sanctuary of Pompeii, thereby contributing to the start of a "fashion" which still continues today. During the 17th century this "fashion" was nurtured by discoveries in Rome and Naples such as the altar of Isis (1605), followed by "Egyptian" discoveries in Naples (the statue of the Nile, the Apis ox) and in Pozzuoli (the statue of Serapis). The excavation site which uncovered the Pompeian sanctuary revealed a genuine Egyptian temple, complete with its sculptural furnishings and painted decorations. The news of this discovery brought artists and travellers from the whole of Europe to the site. They were all fascinated by the magnificent designs and cult objects,which served to reconstruct, both on paper and in reality, the atmospherie rites and ceremonies soon to be adopted by the newly-formed Freemasonry as the symbol of universal re-birth. These same beliefs were the reason behind the choice of the young Mozart to use the architecture of the Pompeian sanctuary which he had visited during his Italian travels (1769-70), as the stage scenery for the Viennese premiere of his opera *The Magic Flute*, which was also inspired by the Isian creed. Cork models of the temple made by Neapolitan artists also contributed to its fame, the most famous of which was commissioned by the King of Sweden. A porcelain table service made by the Royal Factory of Capodimonte, a gift to the Duchess of Parma from the King of Naples, was decorated with designs taken from the ornaments of the Pompeian temple. This seventeenth-century myth which saw Egypt as a symbol of a re-birth, was destined to wane during the next century.
The overwhelming power of Christianity soon suffocated this myth, as is shown by the novel *The Last Days of Pompeii* written by E. Bulwer Lytton and published in 1834, which was inspired by a different concept which contrasted the vision of a "beautiful and pure" Greece with an "evil and corrupt" Egypt. This outlook influenced successive works as well and contributed significantly to the "silence" maintained by scientific literature which ignored the Pompeian sanctuary.
Fortunately, however, the Herculanean Academy documented the sanctuary by dedicating ninety copper engravings to the sanctuary which are today preserved in the collections of the Museum.

The Religion of the Vesuvian cities

Statue of Apollo shooting an arrow, from Pompeii

Gold oil lamp, from the Temple of Venus in Pompeii

A specific section of the display will be reserved to illustrate the cults of the Vesuvian cities as documented by the public and private monuments found in the excavations. The two statues representing the shooting Apollo and Artemis belonged to the central Temple of Apollo, and they derived from original Greek ones which illustrated the killing of the Niobids, the sons and daughters of Niobe; the gold oil lamp belonged to the Sanctuary of Venus near Porta Marina where it was offered to the goddess by Nero and Poppaea. From the Temple of Aesculapius on Via di Stabia, incorrectly referred to as the Temple of Jupiter Meilichios, come the two clay statues representing the god of medicine and his companion Hygeia, together with the bust of Athena which may have belonged to a cult place dedicated to the goddess which no longer exists. There is much richer evidence for the domestic *lararium* (the place reserved in the home for the cult of the Lares, traditional minor gods), with numerous statues of Mercury, Hercules, and Fortune, together with the comforting personifications of the Genii and the familiar Lares. There is also evidence of oriental cults: the Phrygian Sabatius, the Egyptian triad of Isis, Anubis and Arpocrates, and the Trojan Cybele.

Bronze Votive Hand of Sabatius, from Herculaneum

Statuettes of Lares, from the House of the Golden Cupid, Pompeii

Scale model of Pompeii

This scale model was commissioned by Giuseppe Fiorelli and carried out for the most part between 1861 and 1864 by Felice Padiglioni. It reproduced the buildings of Pompeii excavated up until 1879 at a scale of 1:100. This work belonged to a craft tradition of extremely high quality, introduced to the Royal Bourbonic Museum by his father Domenico Padiglioni, who was responsible for the wooden and cork models of the temples of Paestum, the Colosseum and several buildings in Pompeii which were originally displayed in a special room of the Picture Gallery in Naples.

The materials used for the model of Pompeii, which has recently undergone a careful and elaborate restoration, included: ply-wood (for the base of the buildings and the streets); cork (for the walls of the buildings) which has been incised to reproduce the different techniques of ancient buildings; plaster; paper (for the paintings and the floors).

The importance of historical documentation is evident, especially regarding the wall and floor decorations which are modelled with extraordinary delicacy and incredible precision.

Vesuvian Painting

This is one of the most renowned collections of the Neapolitan Museum due both to the richness of the evidence it provides, as well as the fame that followed the unearthing of the Vesuvian cities. It was organised at the beginning of this century according to chronological and thematic criteria; this layout has remained unaltered even today, except for changes made in the arrangement of several important groups.
Except for the paintings of the so-called First Style left in the houses because they were not illustrated, the Neapolitan collection documents the evolution of Roman pictorial styles from the late Republic to the Empire, from the theatrical scenes of the Villa of Publius Fannio Synistor of Boscoreale, right up to the mythological or landscape paintings which were so popular at the beginning of the Empire. The Fourth Style section is particularly rich, dating back to the last phase of the Vesuvian cities and well-illustrated by a number of works: these include the large paintings found in the Basilica of Herculaneum which celebrate the myths of the foundation and the illustrious genealogies of the city, the picture gallery inspired by Homeric subjects found in the House of the Tragic Poet, the refined friezes representing cupids at work from the House of the Deer of Herculaneum and the small whimsical still-life paintings found in Pompeian homes.

Male and female Centaurs from the so-called Villa of Cicero in Pompeii

Roman Painting and the Pompeian Styles

"The ancients who inaugurated the use of wall decorations at first imitated the variegated appearance and arrangement of marbled stuccoes and subsequently the various combinations of wreaths, small pods and leaves. Later on, they began to imitate the shapes of buildings, the protruding reliefs of columns and pediments, tragic, comic and satirical scenic backgrounds were painted in open spaces such as the exedrae, due to the enormous wall space, and decorations depicting various landscapes according to the characteristics of the specific area, were painted in the covered walkways, due to their extensive length. There are paintings of ports, promontories, beaches, rivers, streams, sea straits, sanctuaries, sacred groves, mountains, flocks of sheep, shepherds, while others use megalography *instead of a statue, portraits of divinities, or narration in series of mythological portraits, as well as the battles fought at Troy or the locations of the wanderings of Ulysses and decorative elements which, in the same way as these, have been created by nature.*
These figurative subjects which were implied copies of real elements, today deserve our disapproval because of the diffusion of a depraved style. The walls are painted with monstrosities instead of precise depictions that conform to well – defined objects: instead of columns there are reeds; instead of pediments there are ornamental designs with curled and spiral leaves; there are candelabras bearing images of temples with delicate flowers poking through the pediments, as well as roots coming up through the volutes and in the centre for no reason, there are seated figures; small stems bearing figures divided into two halves, one with a human head and the other with an animal head.
But these figures do not exist, they cannot exist, they have never existed...and yet, people see these deceptions and, instead of criticising them, are delighted without reflecting if they could possibly exist in reality or not."
This is what Vitruvius (VII, 5, 1ss.) wrote in regard to the pictorial styles of the ancients, from the end of the 2nd century B.C. to the Augustan age, in the well-known passage which has influenced all the specialised studies of modern times, and which is considered the basis of the chronological division of the four Pompeiian styles.

Tightrope-walking Silenuses from the so-called Villa of Cicero in Pompeii

First Style

Also known as "encrustation" or "structural" style, it imitates an isodomic structure made of blocks of marble by means of panels in polychromatic stucco. It is of Greek origin and was frequently used throughout the 2nd century B.C.

Second Style

Also known as "architectural" style, it is characterised by the use of paintings in perspective and the division of the wall into the dado, the middle zone which contains architectural elements, and the upper zone with fake porticoes, colonnaded halls and theatrical backdrops. It remained in use throughout the 1st century B.C. until the beginning of the Imperial age.

Third Style

Also known as "ornamental", it abandons the fake perspectives of the preceding style and introduces decorative systems (thin columns, candelabras) divided according to the same scheme (dado, middle zone and upper zone) and framing a central area which contains mythological scenes. Typical of the Augustan age, the style was used until the first half of the 1st century A.D.

Fourth Style

Also known as "fantastic" style, it re-introduces the architectural elements of the Second Style in compositions which are far richer and more complex: on the panels of the medial zone, which are framed by typical borders, there are isolated figures or mythological scenes. This style was developed from the middle of the 1st century A.D onwards.

Megalography from the Villa of Publius Fannio Synistor in Boscoreale

Part of the sumptuous painted decoration of the villa, which is one of the best preserved examples of the Second Style, is housed in the Museum of Naples. One preserved section, which includes part of the decoration of the triclinium, centred on a monumental door with panelled shutters, culminating in a frieze depicting hunting scenes which re-evoke the Macedonian tombs of the Hellenistic age. Another example is part of the decoration of the *oecus* made up of the famous megalography portraying historical subjects. The painted panels, framed by monumental ashlar columns

and culminating in a Doric frieze behind which is a colonnade shown in perspective, represent two figures facing each other: the figure in the foreground, wearing a Persian headdress, may represent Persia or Asia; the identity of the second figure is still uncertain. Some believe it refers to a Hellenistic prince (Antigonus Gonatas, Antigonus Doson, Demetrius Poliorketes), whereas others argue it is a Macedonian allegory which explains both the *kausia*, characteristic Macedonian headdress fixed by a regal band, as well as the large shield with an eight-pointed star in the centre. The figure of the old man leaning on a stick and looking at the two seated figures has been identified as either a philosopher or a wise seer.

Flora, from the Villa of Varano also known as the Villa of Ariadne, in Castellammare di Stabia

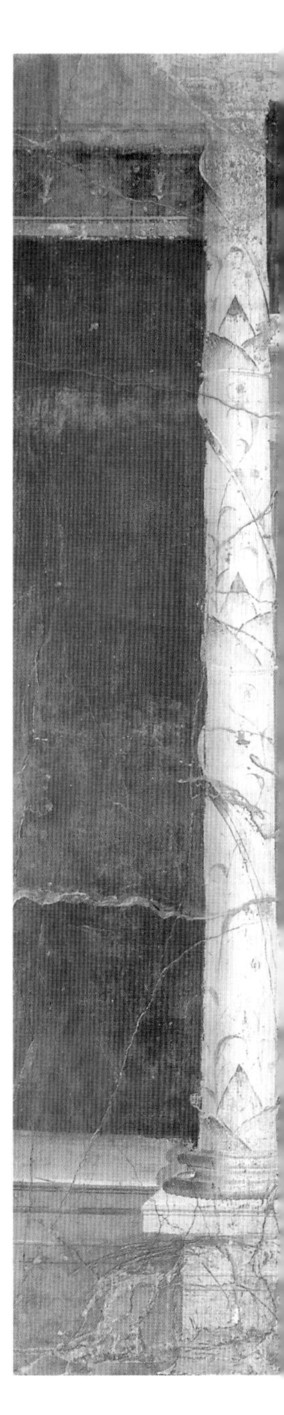

Architecture in green monochrome, from a villa near the Royal Stables in Portici

Landscape paintings

"We must give credit to Studius, who lived during the Augustan age and was the first to invent the graceful style of painting the walls with images of country homes, ports, landscape themes, sacred groves, woods, hills, fish ponds, canals, rivers, beaches, according to the wishes of each patron. In each of these paintings, he included various types of people who are either walking or navigating, or travelling towards their villa by land, donkey or cart, or fishing or hunting or even gathering grapes. Among his painting subjects, there are also noble country homes which can be reached by crossing marshes, and women being carried by hired carriers, caracoling on the shoulders of the trembling porters, as well as many other similar refinements represented with exquisite wit. The same painter began painting maritime cities on outdoor walls, beautiful works of art which cost very little" (Pliny the Elder, Natural History, 35, 116-117). Landscape scenery, almost always of a sacred nature, became popular in the Third Style paintings, as seen in contemporary reliefs, exemplifying the climate of peace and prosperity established with the coming of the new era and spread by court poetry (Virgil, Propertius).

Maritime landscape, from Stabiae

Small paintings representing architectural landscapes, from Pompeii

Sacred landscape, from Pompeii

Garden Paintings

The garden, in addition to royal vestibules, atriums and peristyles, appears to be one of the characteristics, suggested by Vitruvius (VI, 5, 2), for the homes of people holding public appointments: from the late Republic onwards, as documented by literary sources and to a lesser extent by archaeological ones, the sacred groves (*silvae*) and covered walkways (*ambulationes*) abounding in exotic plants and ornaments, decorated city dwellings as they once did the suburban villas (so much so that Cicero, after restoring his house on the Palatine Hills, did not feel the need to go out into the country), according to a fashion that initiated the magnificent residences of Hellenistic princes. At the same time, the custom of painting gardens on the walls of living rooms or on the end walls of open spaces became popular. They were characterised by evergreen plants in perpetual bloom, inhabited by birds and enriched by sculptures which reflected, as did the royal gardens, social prestige and the need of the master of the house to show off.
This genre, which may first have been used, inaugurated perhaps in the subterranean hall of the Villa of Livia at Prima Porta in Rome (today housed in the National Museum at Rome in Palazzo Massimo alle Terme), experienced immense popularity as documented by examples from the Vesuvian cities, ranging from the pictures of *horti conclusi* found on the Third Style walls to the megalographics with exotic animals of later paintings.

Detail of a fresco depicting a garden, from Pompeii

Still life Paintings

Pliny the Elder recalls an artist from the end of the 4th century B.C. by the name of Pireikos who, "though he was second to none as far as art was concerned, must be distinguished because despite dealing always with humble subjects, nonetheless he attained glory in the field of humility. He painted barbershops and shoemakers, donkeys, food and the like, and for this reason he was called *rhyparographos*. On the other hand, he demonstrated his ability and determination with these subjects and his works were sold at a higher price than the greater works of many others" (*Natural History*, 35, 112). This type of painting was later copied by Poxis, a Greek terracotta potter, perhaps from Magnesia on the Meandres, who was active in Rome during the late Republican period. Marcus Varro recounts having met and admired him for his paintings of fruit, grapes and fish, painted in such a realistic way as not to be able to distinguish them from the originals (Pliny the Elder, *Natural History*, 35, 155). Vitruvius explains that the small still-life paintings derive from a Greek tradition of offering to one's guests, the day after a dinner invitation, chickens, eggs, vegetables, fruits and other agricultural products, which is why the term *xenia* (guest gifts) is applied to them (VI, 7, 4).
As previously documented in Second Style paintings with small pictures being placed on shelves on the upper part of the walls or isolated architectural scenes, this genre continued right into the next style. Miniature representations on columns, baseboards and the *predelle* of Third Style walls became larger until they substituted the paintings depicting mythological scenes which were found in the centre of Fourth Style walls.

Mosaic with fish and ducks, from Pompeii

Still life from the Villa of Julia Felix (Pompeii, II,4,3)

Architecture with tholos and still life from Pompeii, House VI, Insula Occidentalis, 41

Painting representing Hercules and Telephus from Herculaneum, Basilica

The painting found in the Basilica of Herculaneum is a copy of the famous painting by Apelles, "Hercules turning around", from the Roman Temple of Diana on the Aventine, as mentioned by Pliny. It represents the Greek hero watching the marvel of a doe suckling his child Telephus. The scene is completed by a seated personification of Arcadia with a basket loaden with fruit, the eagle of Zeus Olympus and the lion of Nemea. The episode of the suckling of Telephus, which was also represented on the altar of Pergamon to exalt the mythical origins of the city and dynasty of the Attalids, has very strong connections with the Roman legend of the she-wolf nursing the twin founders of Rome, justified by the same Trojan origins of both peoples (the Romans and the Pergamenes). This legend was disseminated from the start of the 2nd century, as shown by the oldest decoration of the Temple of Apollonis of Cizico (representing Romulus and Remus) and the panels from Campania of later date, which unite the myths of Telephus and the twin founders of Rome.

The Basilica of Herculaneum also contained other great works with mythological subjects (Theseus the liberator, Achilles and Chiron, Marsyas and Olympus). The choice of subject matter for the decorations of the Basilica is almost certainly connected to the myths regarding the founding of the Vesuvian city that had elected Hercules as its eponymous hero, and to the policy of religious restoration promoted by the Flavian emperors which concentrated on themes regarding the origins of Rome. The legend of Hercules' son also inspired the neo-Attic relief found in the house in Herculaneum known as the relief of Telephus, now in the Museum of Naples.

The Prehistoric and Protohistoric Section

The Museum's collection is the result of research carried out in Southern Italy and, in particular, in Grotta Pertosa and the necropolis of Murgia Timone in Matera by Giovanni Patroni, a real pioneer in this field. Along with the documentation collected in those excavations, artefacts from the pre-Hellenistic necropolis of Cumae and the tombs of the Sarno Valley were soon added to this material (1901-1904). This research was followed by the work carried out by Ugo Rellini in the Grotta delle Felci in Capri, and by Italo Sgobbo at Ariano Irpino and Mirabella Eclano. During World War II, soldiers of the Allied Forces discovered an important group of vases in the protohistoric necropolis of Gaudo in Paestum.

In 1950, Giorgio Buchner re-organised the collection, which had meanwhile been enriched by the magnificent Spinelli Collection (around 7000 objects from the Suessula necropolis), and the grave goods of the Gaudo Culture discovered in the Materdei district of Naples.
New excavations were commissioned by the Superintendency in the necropolis of Capua, the necropolis of Calatia, on the Isle of Vivara, and in other ancient settlements of Campania.
The present-day collection is the result of a very recent re-organisation of the collection which finished in 1995. The artefacts are displayed on two different levels: the first is horizontal, of a topographic nature, allowing one to follow diachronically the development of each single culture in Campania from prehistory to the threshold of

Cup on high pedestal with figures representing "the lord of the horses", from Capua

Coarse ware vessel, from Capri

Figulina ware vessel with flame decoration, from Capri

The village of Vivara in Procida

In ancient times, the islet of Vivara was probably joined to Procida: the excavations carried out at the end of the 1970s, preceded by the research of Giorgio Buchner in Punta Capitello before World War II (1937), have resulted in the discovery of two settlements dating back to the Middle Bronze Age (16th - 14th centuries B.C.) located in Punta di Mezzogiorno and Punta d'Alaca. The houses were oval-shaped huts with the area around them delimited by post holes, and with the fireplace in the centre of the hut. Pieces of crucibles and traces of bronze have led to the hypothesis that there was local manufacture of metals. Fragments of imported Mycenaean ceramics dating to the Helladic II A and II B and therefore to the 15th century B.C., attest to the commercial relations with the Aegean world in a period which considerably precedes the ancient Greek colonisation of the Western world.

Greek colonisation; the second is vertical, of a chronological nature, allowing one to "travel" backwards in time from the late Bronze Age back to the Palaeolithic.
Important material from the Lower Palaeolithic comes from Capri: the remains of bears, boars and hippopotamuses remind us of the words of Suetonius regarding Augustus' passion for "rare and ancient objects...discovered in Capri, thought to be the bones of the Giants". Finds dated to the Middle Neolithic (painted pottery with band and flame decoration) and the Bronze Age were also found on the island in the Grotta delle Felci.
Examples of the Copper Age Gaudo Culture come from the grave goods found in the "rock cut" tombs in Piano di Sorrento and Materdei in Naples. The protohistoric village of Vivara in Procida provides material from the Middle Bronze Age through the discovery of traces of local manufacture of metals and numerous imported Mycenaean ceramics.
The Iron Age is documented by the cremation tombs of Sant'Angelo in Formis, characterised by a biconical cinerary urn tradition, and inhumation burials of the so-called Trench Culture or *Fossakultur* discovered in the Valley of Sarno (Striano, San Marzano, San Valentino Torio), as well as in inland northern Campania (Suessula, Calatia).

Greek Culture in the Bay of Naples

This section is dedicated to the history and the archaeology of the Bay of Naples, from the first commercial exchanges with the Greek world to the foundation of the colonies of *Pithecusae*, Cumae and Naples itself, and finally to the revival of Hellenic styles and customs by the Roman culture and society of the late Republic. This is all excellently exemplified by the Museum's exhibition of the very refined decorative programme of the Villa of the Papyri of Herculaneum.
The artefacts of pre-Hellenic Cumae, where locally produced vases were found in association with the imported Greek geometric vases, are followed by the presentation of the Greek emporium of *Pithecusae*, on the island of Ischia. Pithecusae was the oldest Greek settlement in the Western world, so remote as to be associated in the Hellenic imagination with "a savage island, situated at the ends of the world and inhabited by monkeys". The only evidence of the rich cultural exchanges that the Greek colonists, originally from the island of Euboea, had with the local populations is the wealth of grave goods found in the tombs excavated in the valley of San Montano which today are housed in the Museum of Naples and the new Museum of Villa Arbusto at Lacco Ameno in Ischia.
There is a wealth of documentation regarding the Greek colony of Cumae in the Museum. Cumae was founded some time

Antefix of a human head from the Sanctuary of the goddess Marica in Minturno after Pithecusae by the Euboeians, as confirmed by the sporadic archaeological investigation of the 17th century, and continued more systematically during the second half of the 1800s and the first decades of the 1900s by Giuseppe Fiorelli, Enrico Stevens, Giovanni Pellegrini and Ettore Gabrici.

The collection of material from Cuma is followed by the section dedicated to Naples which contains material from the earliest Greek settlement of Parthenope, discovered in the necropolis of Pizzofalcone dating to somewhere between the 7th century and the 6th century B.C., and the finds from the "new city" (Neapolis) which, according to legend, was founded around 475 B.C. by the inhabitants of the island of Ischia which had been placed under the political control of Syracuse and the city of Cumae. Confirmation of what has been handed down by literary sources is provided by the wealth of funerary artefacts from the necropolis of Castelcapuano exhibited together with the more recent findings from the necropolis of Santa Teresa excavated during the 1800s and which have mostly been lost. There is plenty of evidence for cult activity in Neapolis; a magnificent votive deposit was found on the hill of Sant'Aniello in Caponapoli (on the site of the ancient acropolis) made up of over 700 votive terracottas which probably came from the Sanctuary of Demeter; further evidence is provided by the statues of the Dioscuri from the temple of the Dioscuri in the *agora* (market place in the very heart of the city); the temple was restored at the start of the Empire as a result of the growing imperial cult and later incorporated into the Church of St. Paolo Maggiore.

Lekane lid by the Painter C, from Cumae

Panathenaic-type amphora, from Cumae

THE HOUSE OF PUNTA CHIARITO

A very recent and fruitful excavation has uncovered a small village of huts, dating back to the second half of the 8th century B.C. and buried by a mudslide during the 6th century, on the promontory of Punta Chiarito in the southern part of the island of Ischia. Above all, this is an extraordinary discovery because of the exceptional state of preservation of the village due to a tragic piece of fate which foreshadowed what would happen to nearby Pompeii. In one of the exhibition rooms of the Museum of Naples, a hut from the village has been reconstructed to exemplify Greek domestic architecture in the first phase of the colony's life.

The house had an oval shape, with the entrance being on one of the longer sides and the floor made of beaten earth. Alongside the dry-stone walls were post holes used to insert the poles which held up the roof which was covered with both straight and bent roof tiles in the centre part, and reeds and brushwood on the outer part. The spatial layout inside was as follows: a storage room for foodstuffs (situated just inside the entrance), a kitchen with a fireplace and a bedroom on the upper floor. The storage room revealed mainly large containers (amphorae and pithoi) either of local production or Greek and Etruscan imports, as well as cooking ware and fineware found throughout the house. A very interesting discovery was an unfinished vase containing lumps of bronze which probably served as a precious metal for commercial exchanges, given that money was not yet used in this period. The numerous imported vases were almost all in some way connected to the Greek banquet ritual: a Laconian crater, Ionic cups, Corinthian craters, bronze basins with a pearled border, and graters. Fishing gear (bronze fishhooks and lead weights for the nets), farming equipment (sickles, pickaxes), a few weapons (the tip of a spear and a sword), and loomweights used for female domestic activities, were all found in the kitchen near the hearth.

Votive reliefs dedicated to the nymphs

A series of marble votive reliefs were found in a sanctuary dedicated to the nymphs built in Barano, on the island of Ischia, near a spring that still flows today. The reliefs are inscribed in Greek and in Latin, and are decorated with the typical seashells testifying to the religiosity of the Roman epoch which was connected to the cult of the waters of more ancient origin.

Attic red figured Pelike representing the birth of Helen from an egg

The painted vase served as a cinerary urn in a tomb which dates to the end of the 5th century B.C. It was found in Naples in Via S. Tommaso d'Aquino and has been attributed to the Painter of Nicia. This vase is one of the oldest known representations of the Greek myth of the birth of Helen from an egg.
There are two known versions of this myth: the first and most ancient is Attic-inspired and it recounts the birth of Helen from the union between Zeus and the goddess Nemesis; the second is based on a Laconian tradition and attributes the conception of the egg to Leda, the wife of Tyndareus, king of Sparta, and loved by Zeus disguised as a swan, as documented by Timoteos' well-known sculptural group. The first version of this myth is

represented on a group of sixteen vases, produced in Attica during the last thirty years of the 5th century B.C., and the Neapolitan *pelike* is part of this group. The decision to represent the period of expectation before the miraculous event when the egg hatches and the Greek heroine is born, is common to all the vases. Leda and Tyndarus are both present together with the divine twins Dioscuri who, in some versions of the myth and in illustrated Roman documents, shared with Helen the birth from an egg fertilised by Zeus.

The painted scene perfectly describes what was already known from written sources regarding the union between Zeus and Nemesis which took place in the sanctuary of the goddess in Ramnunte. According to Iginus' narration, it was Hermes who brought Nemesis' egg to Leda with the order to place it on the altar of the temple on the warm remains of the sacrifice that would cause the egg to hatch; according to Sappho, Leda found the egg in a swamp. The version of the myth which tells of Nemesis' egg falling from the moon alludes to the astral nature of the divine *trigemini* (triplets) often characterised by the crescent moon or the torch-bearer (Helen), and the rising morning star or the setting evening star (Castor and Pollux).

Statue of the Black Fisherman

The statue belongs to the genre of sculptures which was particularly appreciated by the rich Romans as decorations for their villas designed for leisure. It is probably an Imperial copy of an original Hellenistic statue from the Alexandrian school. It was found on the island of Gaiola and was part of the sumptuous furnishings of the *Pausilypon*, the famous villa of Vedius Pollio, which was later inherited by Augustus and passed into the Imperial domain. The villa was so beautiful and luxurious as to be considered the remedy for all worries.

Villa of the Papyri in Herculaneum

Statue of a drunken Satyr

The villa was the home of a rich and scholarly representative of the late Republican Roman *nobilitas* (perhaps Lucius Calpurnius Piso, father-in-law of Julius Caesar and consul in the year 58 B.C., or his son who was consul in 15 B.C., or possibly Appius Claudius Pulcher, brother-in-law of Lucullus and consul in 38 B.C.); it has produced an extraordinary collection of works of art (50 marble sculptures and 21 bronze ones) and an ample library of Greek and Latin papyri (1,758 rolls). Only a part of the architectural structure is known because of the underground passages built by the Bourbons during the mid-1700s. In order to further our knowledge of what still remains, we must wait for the results of new excavations still in progress. Two statues of Fauns belonged in the atrium, one a dancer and the other a musician with a *tibia*; a series of busts of Greek scholars and a statue of Athena Promachos came from the tablinum; five bronze statues of the Danaides and two hermas of Amazon and Doryphoros by Polycleitus belonged to one of the peristyles. Busts of famous men (kings, strategists, philosophers) decorated the larger peristyle; the furnishings in the garden were dedicated to the colourful and varied world of Dionysus and the Greek culture of the gymnasium, including the statue of a drunken Satyr, the "Hermes at rest" by Lysippus, and two statues of runners.

The daughters of Danaus

The five female bronze statues, considered to be "dancers" by Winckelmann, have recently been recognised as the daughters of Danaus, condemned to having to perpetually pour water as a punishment for having murdered their bridegrooms and their cousins at their father's instigation because he wanted to revenge himself on his brother Egypt. The most famous representation of this theme are the fifty statues of the girls together with fifty statues of their bridegrooms on horseback, which adorned the portico of the Roman Temple of Apollo Palatine, symbolising the victory of Augustus over Egypt after the Battle of Actius. The "dancers" of Herculaneum, which probably served a similar function, were classical copies of "severe style" sculptures and originally were probably positioned in the spaces between the columns of the small peristyle of the Villa (possibly dedicated to Apollo).

Epicurus

The bronze bust of the philosopher has been identified by its inscription in Greek lettering. It is one of a number of Roman copies of an original which historians believe was made immediately after the death of Epicurus (270 B.C.). Its presence in the Villa is not surprising: the philosophical ideals of the owner were all based on Epicurean teaching which taught that life should be full of joy and pleasure and free from pain and worries; this philosophy was so far removed from the

principles of the *polis* that those who followed it were called "those of the garden" (Sextus Empiricus, *Against Mathematicians*, 1, 64).

Pseudo-Seneca

Long thought by the archaeologists to be the portrait of Seneca, the bronze bust from the Villa of the Papyri definitely represents one of the most famous Greek poets (associated at least once with the playwright Menander), realistically characterised by "poor" and "age-worn" features (a face that expresses weariness for the sufferings of day-to-day living and hard work, but illuminated by an interior force and a noble intellect),

very similar to the Hellenistic portrayals of farmers and fishermen. It is an Augustan copy of a statue made around 200 B.C.

HERMES AT REST

This bronze sculpture, representing Hermes at rest, is part of the furnishings of the grand peristyle, characterised by sophisticated references to Dionysian religiosity and the ideals of the Greek gymnasium. It is a Roman copy of a Hellenistic original inspired by Lysippus' prototype. The facial features, which were probably restored in ancient times, recall the characteristics of the portraits of the late Republic and the early Empire, suggesting that it was produced locally: fortunately, it was returned to the Museum collections in 1947 after being stolen from the Montecassino bomb shelter during the war.

Etruscans and Italic peoples in Campania

In spite of the great quantity of material discovered during the 18th and 19th centuries throughout the region (especially in Nola, S. Maria Capua Vetere, Trebula, Cales, Allifae, Teano), it is only on account of the research carried out during this century that it has been possible to reconstruct the history and material culture of the non-Greek cities of ancient Campania populated by Etruscans, Samnites and Campanians

A shield depicting the head of Medusa

From the plundering which occurred during the past centuries, keeping the antique and collectors' markets alive throughout Europe, the Museum of Naples has conserved the main parts of private collections (Mastrilli Museum, Santangelo Collection, Spinelli Collection) displayed together with the material from more recent excavations, in order to offer a more complete picture of the various sites and cultures. For a further study of these subjects, it is well worth visiting the recently established museums in the area.

Vivenzio Hydria

The name was given by the collector who found it in Nola in 1797; the hydria (water vessel) made by the painter of Kleophrade depicts episodes from the legend of Troy which refer to the night preceding the destruction of the city and the escape of Aeneas to the Western world, such as the killing of Priam and Astianax by Neoptolemos, and the kidnapping of Cassandra near the simulacrum of the Palladium. This vase served as a luxurious cinerary urn placed within a large jar together with five alabaster unguentaria and a gem engraved with the eagle of Zeus holding a snake in its claws.

The Weapons of Pietrabbondante

The federal sanctuary of Pietrabbondante in Samnium had an important political and religious function within the ambit of the entire Pentra community and it has produced a great number of bronze and iron weapons (helmets, jaw protectors, shield ornaments, sword-belts, shin protectors), discovered

during the excavations of the previous century and today displayed in the Museum of Naples. For the most part they are probably the spoils taken from enemies which were then offered by the Samnite leaders to the gods after a victory.

The tomb of the Warrior

The tomb of the Warrior, acquired from the Royal Neapolitan collections during the 18th century, has long been thought to originate from one of the Lucanian necropolis of Paestum. Recent study of several documents has disproved this and has fortunately permitted the reconstruction of the original context: it was an elegant tomb, dating to the end of the 4th century B.C., found in the city of Nola. Several formal and iconographic characteristics of the painting had already indicated the artistic production of this city. The same subject matter is represented on both of the longer panels of the tomb: on the better preserved sides, a female figure offers a *skyphos* (cup) to armed men who are coming towards her on foot or on horseback; on the right, the procession is completed by a barefoot equerry who holds the tail of the horse ahead of him. On the shorter panels, there is a horseman with a trophy and a table with gold *hydriai* (water vessels) and a silver *oinochoe* (jug) on it.
This iconography, which was well-known in the tombs of Paestum, refers to the "return of the warrior", laden with spoils seized from the enemy, on whom honours and glory are bestowed by the entire community, represented by the female figure who serves as a double reference both to the public and the private sphere.

Magna Graecia

Apulian red figured crater ("Vase of the Persians"), from Canosa

The section dedicated to Greek culture in the Bay of Naples and non-Hellenic cultures in Campania is completed by the display of material from the main sites of Magna Graecia. This material has been acquired by the Museum over the centuries as the result of frequently disorganised and frenetic excavations or the mania of private collectors. The pieces found in the Museum are only a minimal part of what was found during the excavations, and then lost due to the lack of effective conservation laws and the negligence of court officials who were more interested in the results of the excavations of the Vesuvian cities or the Phlegrean Fields. Another explanation for the loss of so much of the heritage of Magna Graecia was the great passion for "Etruscan vases" which began with the rich Hamilton Collection and the refined English porcelains of J. Wedgwood inspired by the originals. It was during this period that large private collections were started and later enlarged by the finds from excavations and clandestine markets, sometimes finding their way into the Royal Collections: the most important of these was the Santangelo Collection acquired by the Museum in 1865. The establishment of provincial museums, an idea put forward in vain by Michele Arditi back in 1808, as well as the creation of autonomous superintendencies, brought an end to the introduction of artefacts from Magna Graecia into the Museum of Naples, hopefully ending once and for all one of the most embarassing periods for national archaeology.

Cork models of the Temples of Paestum

The section dedicated to Magna Graecia begins with a display of the cork models of the Temples of Paestum, made between 1805 and 1822 by Domenico Padiglioni for the Royal Bourbonic Museum. The fashion for making scale models of the temples began during the years immediately following the "rediscovery" of the ancient city, and continued right through the 19th century, as shown by the *Presepe* (traditional Nativity figures) in the Temple of Neptune, today displayed in the Neapolitan Museum of San Martino. The models were based on drawings, sketches and reliefs made by architects who visited Paestum; their work has certainly contributed to the fortune of this genre which has produced a wealth of documents today divided among the main European collections.

Bronze hydria from Locri

This splendid bronze hydria (water vessel) which dates back to the 5th century B.C., comes from Locri Epizefiri and is now housed in the Museum of Naples.
The decorations of the handles are especially noteworthy: at the bottom of the vertical handle is the head of a bearded Gorgon with wings and folded arms, and moving horses on the side; the top, where the handle is attached to the jug, is decorated by a lion's head; the horizontal handles have palmette attachments and a pair of nude *kouroi* (boys) on opposite sides.

The dancers of Ruvo

These famous paintings, which entered the Royal Collections of Naples in 1838, were discovered five years earlier in a tomb at Ruvo in Puglia with no grave goods other than a figure vase of exquisite workmanship. The damage caused to the frescoes during their discovery, though it prevented sale on the antiquarian market, has undoubtedly hindered full understanding of the monument. It has also raised a number of doubts regarding the sequence of the female figures and the number of male ones. The *chorus* of women holding hands brings to mind, at a mythological level, the merry dance that Theseus and the young Athenians performed in Crete to celebrate the death of the Minotaur. If, however, as in our case, it refers to a funerary context, they allude directly to the social and political prestige of the departed. Furthermore, the adoption of an Attic-inspired theme in an Apulian burial towards the end of the 5th century reflects the political events of those years, during which Athens collaborated with the indigenous centres of Puglia in order to stop the dangerous increase in power of Tarantum.

Figure vases from the Santangelo collection

The Santangelo Collection, so sumptuous as to deserve the name of "museum" on its own, was the superb embellishment of the noble Palazzo Carafa in Naples (the palazzo with the bronze head of a horse donated to Diomede Carafa by Lorenzo de' Medici). The most famous pieces of this collection are the *rhytà* (drinking vessels), rarities in terms of their form and quality of decoration, of which about seventy were displayed in the final section of the collection of antique vases. Their shapes vary, and include a ram's head, a cow's head, "a black man and a crocodile", "a pygmy and a crane", a horse's head, a lamb's head, a Maltese dog's head, and many others. This production covers the period from the middle of the 5th century to the end of the 4th century B.C.

Selected bibliography

A. Ruesch, *Guida illustrata del Museo Nazionale di Napoli*, Napoli 1908.
O. Elia, *Pitture murali e mosaici nel Museo Nazionale di Napoli*, Roma 1932.
L. Breglia, *Catalogo delle oreficerie del Museo Nazionale di Napoli*, Napoli 1941.
R. Siviero, *Gli ori e le ambre del Museo Nazionale di Napoli*, Napoli 1954.
A. de Franciscis, *Il Museo Nazionale di Napoli*, Cava dei Tirreni-Napoli 1963.
Da Palazzo degli Studi a Museo Archeologico. Catalogo della mostra storico-documentaria del Museo Nazionale di Napoli, Napoli 1977.
La collezione egiziana del Museo Archeologico Nazionale di Napoli, Napoli 1989.
M. Borriello, R. Cantilena (*et alii*), *Le collezioni del Museo Nazionale di Napoli*, 2 vol., Roma 1986 e 1989.
Alla ricerca di Iside. Analisi, studi e restauri dell'Iseo pompeiano nel Museo di Napoli, Napoli 1992.
S. De Caro, *Il Museo Archeologico Nazionale di Napoli*, Napoli 1994.
C. Gasparri, *Le gemme Farnese*, Napoli 1994.
M. Borriello, S. De Caro, *La Magna Grecia nelle collezioni del Museo Archeologico di Napoli*, Napoli 1996.
S. De Caro, *Il Museo Archeologico Nazionale di Napoli. Guida alle collezioni*, Napoli 1999.

Printed in September 2001
on behalf of Electa Napoli

Photocomposition
Grafica Elettronica, Naples
Photolithograph and printing
SAMA, Naples